This book belongs to

T0326687

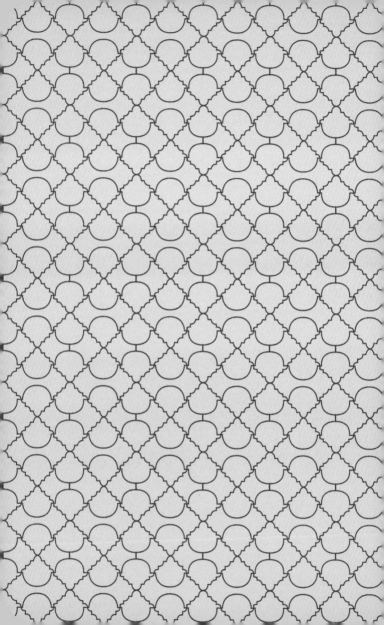

10 PRAYER SECRETS

10 PRAYER SECRETS

Supernatural Power for Your Breakthrough

HAKEEM COLLINS

Chosen

a division of Baker Publishing Group
Minneapolis, Minnesota

Published by Chosen Books
11400 Hampshire Avenue South
Bloomington, Minnesota 55438
www.chosenbooks.com

Chosen Books is a division of
Baker Publishing Group, Grand Rapids, Michigan

Printed in China

ISBN 978-0-8007-9971-7

Library of Congress Cataloging-in-Publication Control Number: 2020931295

Cover design by Dan Pitts

20 21 22 23 24 25 26   7 6 5 4 3 2 1

CONTENTS

PART 2: 30 DAYS OF PRAYER FOR BREAKTHROUGH

INTRODUCTION

The secrets contained in this book are for those who are tired of prayers as usual and desire to see God's supernatural power released for breakthrough. Because you are reading these words, I know that God wants to take your prayers to new heights, realms and possibilities.

I have divided this book into two sections. Part 1 contains inspirational teaching on ten biblical prayer secrets that will revolutionize your connection to God and your prayer life. The theme of each prayer secret in part 1 continues in part 2, which contains thirty days of questions for reflection or journaling, Scripture for additional study, powerful prayer declarations and daily activations for personal prayer growth in your life. You may want to read the book in order from start to finish, or consider reading a chapter from part 1 and then turning to the three devotionals in part 2 that correspond to that specific prayer secret. I know this book will make a profound difference in the way you approach God in prayer and the results you see when you pray.

Get ready to explore ten prayer secrets that are hope-filled, practical and biblical to bring you to a place of personal breakthrough. Prayer is not a boring recitation of words but supernatural communication with the God of miracles! God bless you as you hear the Word and put it into practice. Your breakthrough is on the way.

Dr. Hakeem Collins

PART 1

10 PRAYER SECRETS

DISCOVER YOUR PASSION

God places His heart in ours, and that God-given passion can serve as fuel for prayer.

Whatever you do, work heartily, as for the Lord and not for men.

COLOSSIANS 3:23 ESV

Imagine having an eight-year-old son who, like most little boys, loves playing with cars and trucks. He envisions becoming a NASCAR winner one day. What are you likely to buy him for his birthday or Christmas? Will you get him a hammer and nails because you want him to grow up to be a carpenter? I would imagine not. As a parent you would give him what he is passionate about. What he loves and enjoys the most.

What father or mother would say, "Son, here's a toolbox because I want you to develop a passion to be a mechanic"? Your role as a parent is not to extinguish his dreams, aspirations and purpose in life but to empower him to distinguish for himself what he wants to become and to pursue it passionately.

Do you recall your childhood dreams and what you wanted to be when you grew up? I wanted to be a lawyer or a judge. We all dreamed about becoming something special in life, whether it was a doctor, nurse, artist, entrepreneur, author, athlete or maybe a mother or father with a beautiful family. But then life happened. Some of us were told our dreams were unrealistic or not practical. Imagine yourself as that eight-year-old child being told, "Be realistic with your dreams. It's impossible to become a NASCAR winner."

God's Predestined Plans

Maybe as that eight-year-old you thought you heard the voice of God talking to you in the still of the night—calling you to a particular kind of life or a unique occupation. So, what happened? Along the way, for most of us, in our attempts to be realistic, practical and responsible adults, we grew out of touch with our creative, innovative side to dream wildly. Ultimately, we gave up on our commitment to translate our God-given dreams into purpose-driven reality.

It does not need to be that way. All of us, no matter how old we are or what kind of profession we occupy, can learn to bring that authentic, unique, childlike creativity forth in prayer.

Each one of us has a purpose given by God and revealed to us in prayer. God says it this way: "I know what I'm doing. I have it all planned out—plans to take care of you, not abandon you, plans to give you the future you hope for" (Jeremiah 29:11 Message). The Bible also says that "we are God's [own] handiwork (His workmanship), recreated in Christ Jesus, [born anew] that we may do those good works which God predestined (planned beforehand) for us . . . that we should walk in them [living the good life which He prearranged and made ready for us to live]" (Ephesians 2:10 AMPC).

God gives each one of us gifts, talents, abilities and a divine purpose; He wants us to fulfill what we were created for. He wants us to discover or rediscover the good works He has for us to do. This is why heartfelt prayer is vital to unlocking our hidden potential and the passion that drives it. Prayer comes alive and becomes a place where dreams are revealed and take shape. Every purpose needs passion to fuel it.

If you are to fulfill your God-given dreams, you must start by asking the right questions. Rather than focus on all the things you want when you pray, consider seeking what He desires for you. As you begin to discover His clear purpose for your life, you will find yourself pursuing it eagerly. You will gain wisdom from the Holy Spirit to fulfill the future He has promised you (see Proverbs 19:21).

Most people are going in circles in life like a dog chasing its tail, getting themselves dizzy and confused about what God has called them to do. Prayer will bring the matters of the heart to the surface. It is, after all, what we hold in our hearts that God is after when we pray! Matthew 6:21 (ESV) declares: "Where your treasure is, there your heart will be also." We value only what we hold dear. Never pursue a dream that your heart is not passionate about.

Purposely Passionate

Passion often separates success from failure. One of the most powerful weapons on earth is the believer who discovers her passion in prayer and uses it to bring her God-given purpose into fruition. The questions that many of us have on our hearts—*What is my purpose in life? What do I really care about?*—are answered in the prayer room where God speaks to us concerning them.

God uses our emotions and longings—those things that move, stir or frustrate us—to get our attention. This is the language of passion, and it helps identify the specific call He is highlighting. Not only do we discover our passion in prayer, but discovering our passion will also help us pray.

God wants us to find a point of passion that sets our prayers on fire. He is not waiting to hear lethargic prayers but rather passionate ones from people whose hearts are set ablaze by something they love . . . or are dissatisfied about. We can accomplish much when we are filled with passion.

Passion is like a candle that burns, and its aroma fills the room. Passion, burning on the inside, can affect everything on the outside. God wants you to locate that one thing that burns in your heart and use it to fuel your prayer life in order to achieve the results you seek. This applies not only to the big picture, such as finding your call in life, but also to prayer concerns you face every day. Suppose, for example, you are praying for someone you love who needs a healing breakthrough. Your prayers, motivated by your passion, will carry the heartfelt burden, consistency and empathy needed to pray earnestly until you see supernatural breakthrough.

God wants us to align our passion with His will, which He puts into our hearts, and then pray until we see results (see Matthew 21:22; 1 John 5:14). I believe prayers are answered when we pray for something that moves, upsets and drives us. God partners with our fiery passion to ignite the change we are praying for.

Burdened with Purpose

Prayer is key to unleashing this kind of passion. As we bring our burdens to prayer, the Lord gives us the plans of action we need as well as the passion to fulfill them. Knowledge is valuable, but passion is invaluable. In our spiritual journeys, prayer is key to activating the inner drive necessary to fulfill our God-given dreams and live blessed and prosperous lives in Christ.

When God speaks to us, His messages burn in our hearts like fire. The prophet Jeremiah experienced this. When he wanted to stop prophesying because his messages from the Lord were ruining his reputation, Jeremiah exclaimed, "If I say I'll never mention the LORD or speak in his name, his word burns in my heart like a fire. It's like a fire in my bones! I am worn out trying to hold it in!" (Jeremiah 20:9 NLT). God has this kind of fire for you.

There are three things necessary to start a fire: fuel, oxygen and a spark. The Word of God is our fuel; prayer is our oxygen; and passion is our spark. Jesus prayed passionately and usually found a place of solitude to do so (see Mark 1:35). He prayed all night to choose those who would be with Him in ministry (see Luke 6:12–16). He taught them to pray fervently always (see Luke 18:1).

Likewise, we should pray with passion—as if someone's life depended on it. Our prayers should create holy discontentment to rise up and act! Supernatural breakthroughs occur in our lives only when prayer and burden collide. As the title of an old gospel song puts it, "It's Hard to Stumble (When You're on Your Knees)." God empowers us for our purposes as we kneel before Him. Protect your time with the Father as if your life depended on it—because it really does!

Christian believers can be fervent in spirit (see Romans 12:11) and zealous of good works in all we do (see Titus 2:14), no matter how frigid our spiritual atmospheres have become (see Matthew 22:35–40). Jesus was "eaten up" with passion for the Father (John 2:17 NKJV). Apollos was fervent in spirit when he spoke and taught things of the Lord (see Acts 18:25). The Corinthian believers' fervency and enthusiasm provoked others to good works (see 2 Corinthians 9:2). *Fervent* (*zeō*) means "to boil with heat" (Strong's G2204), which is a good picture of how the fire of our passion can affect our surroundings.

The Reason for Prayer

"Intercession is not a job," says Alice Smith in *Beyond the Veil* (Chosen, 2010). "It's a love relationship developed between you and your heavenly Father. Intercession is a stethoscope to the heart of God." Without passion, prayer becomes stagnant, boring and ineffective. Yet, very few people use the word *passionate* to describe their prayer lives. Instead, many admit to being distracted, bored and frustrated.

Believers fail to experience purposeful prayer lives for one important reason: We misunderstand God's purpose for prayer. Believers and nonbelievers alike have the misconception that prayer is primarily for gain—a time to inform the Lord of our needs. First Peter 2:9 reveals to us that all Christians are called to be of a "royal priesthood." As spiritual priests, therefore, we are called to a life of intercession. If we desire to have a more purposeful prayer life, we must understand that the Lord's reason for giving us prayer goes beyond petitioning Him for our daily personal needs. It encompasses a divine call to become passionate prayer partners with God to establish His will on earth.

DRIVEN TO FULFILL YOUR PASSION

Nehemiah is known primarily for the rebuilding of Jerusalem (see Nehemiah 1:1–11). As cupbearer to a foreign king, Nehemiah was in a position of authority. One day when his brother and some other men were newly arrived from Jerusalem, Nehemiah asked them about the beloved city and the remnant who had survived the exile.

He learned that Jerusalem's wall had crumbled, the gates had been burned and the citizens were in great distress. Upon hearing the news, he mourned, prayed and fasted before God. Then, displaying great courage, he asked the king to allow him to go to Jerusalem to rebuild the wall. Remarkably, Nehemiah harnessed his passion in prayer, letting it drive him as he led the people to reconstruct the massive wall in just 52 days, which restored the city's honor and strength.

Passion is created when a believer embraces a specific burden. Effective leaders always respond with action to the burdens they carry. When Nehemiah asked about the Jews who had survived and now lived back in the province, we see clearly his passion for the people and their spiritual livelihood. Through prayer and fasting Nehemiah moved from a position of being overwhelmed by a problem to passionately developing a solution.

As followers of Jesus—a people of prayer called to love—we should carry our burdens passionately and express them openly. Our passion should be the fuel that motivates us to bring change, not only for us but also for those we are called to serve.

Your prayer life will take on new purpose and power as you partner with God for the things that are on His heart. As you embrace your passion fully to do what God has called you to do, He will bring increase, favor, blessings, wisdom and breakthrough.

Discover your passion in prayer, knowing that it is "God Who is all the while effectually at work in you [energizing and creating in you the power and desire], both to will and to work for His good pleasure and satisfaction and delight" (Philippians 2:13 AMPC).

If you wish, you may turn at this point to part 2, "30 Days of Prayer for Breakthrough," and proceed with Days 1–3. Upon completion you would then return to Secret 2, "Anticipate Your Breakthrough," and follow the directions given for further days of prayer. Or, for a different approach to this book, you might prefer to read all ten secrets first and then enter a thirty-day prayer focus using one devotional for each day.

ANTICIPATE YOUR BREAKTHROUGH

Faith helps us to pray, and prayer gives us faith to anticipate the impossible and lean into our miracles.

> Now faith is confidence in what we hope for and assurance about what we do not see.
>
> HEBREWS 11:1

Faith pleases God, and, in response, He gives us vision to see what only He can do. Think about a time as a child when you asked your parents for a special toy but did not receive it immediately. In fact, you had to look at that toy every time you went to the store. Then when your birthday or Christmas finally came around, you opened your gifts to discover what you had asked for. What excitement you felt to possess what you wanted! The long wait made receiving the gift more special.

There is something powerful about faith when it is activated in prayer to believe God for the unreachable, unattainable, unexplainable or seemingly impossible. Naturally, we would rather have faith in what we see before our eyes. But God's perspective is different: "Faith is the reality of what is hoped for, the proof of what is not seen" (Hebrews 11:1 CSB). Prayer employs our faith to believe God for supernatural things. In other words, believing prayers activate us to foresee what is in the unseen. Prayer gives our faith an assignment to expect, contemplate, predict and reach out for the possibility of our prayers being answered.

God wants us to have faith like the woman who suffered with an issue of blood for twelve years. Her faith to believe that she would be healed before she actually received her healing breakthrough is what I call anticipation. She anticipated being well because she heard that Jesus could heal. She spoke by faith within herself that if she could touch the hem of Jesus' garment, she would be made whole. Her anticipation caused her to reach out toward her miracle, which released healing virtue from Jesus (see Luke 8:40–47).

— Praying Faith —

Prayer works when we work our faith in prayer. Faith helps us to pray, and prayer gives us faith to anticipate the impossible. The Bible says that faith without works is ineffective, useless or dead (see James 2:17), and that we must live by faith and not by sight (see 2 Corinthians 5:7). Faith, therefore, should be a core principle and philosophy for every Christian's spiritual walk. We are not just to pray but rather to pray believing and anticipating (see Matthew 21:22; Mark 11:24–25).

This means, then, that when we pray, we must come praying with faith. A blind beggar named Bartimaeus called out to Jesus for mercy and a miracle. His faith was evident in his public acknowledgment of

Jesus as the Son of God. While the crowd insisted that Bartimaeus be quiet, he became defiantly louder! Jesus instructed His disciples to bring the blind man to Him, and a miracle happened.

Apparently, Bartimaeus did not allow the people to silence or block his faith to receive his miracle breakthrough. He had heard about Jesus' miracles, and his faith to expect what he could not see created a miracle opportunity. If Jesus instructs us specifically to believe when we pray, then it must also be possible to pray and not believe. God is not interested in faithless prayers that lack the anticipation of supernatural outcomes.

Keep this in mind: Not all prayers bring results. Faith-anticipated prayers reach heaven to bring into your reality the supernatural breakthrough you have been expecting. God desires to hear faith-filled prayers that oblige Him "to accomplish infinitely more than we might ask or think" (Ephesians 3:20 NLT).

James 1:6–7 (KJ2000) says, "But let him ask in faith, nothing wavering. For he that wavers is like a wave of the sea driven with the wind and tossed. For let not that man think that he shall receive anything of the Lord." When you pray, are you praying with fear, unbelief or doubt? As believers we can pray with unwavering faith that what we ask of the Father according to His eternal purposes for our lives will manifest (see John 14:14).

Praying with faith is simply communicating with God, believing He hears you and expecting Him to answer you (see 1 John 5:14). Reading, meditating on and declaring the promises of God will strengthen your faith, which will help you lean into your miracle.

— FAITH TO ANTICIPATE —

Why is your anticipation in prayer powerful? In today's culture, the word *anticipation* means little more than a feeling of expectation.

The original sense of *anticipation*, however, had everything to do with preparation and action. Our faith is actually expressed in anticipation. In other words, anticipation is making the preparations and space for what you know is yours by faith. It is getting ready for what the Lord spoke to you during prayer. Noah began constructing the ark—a titanic task—in anticipation of a flood. Hebrews 11:7 states that "by faith Noah, when warned about things not yet seen, in holy fear built an ark to save his family."

Anticipating your breakthrough is like having a group of people gather to pray for rain in a time of drought, and you bring an umbrella. That is anticipation! Anticipation shows up in prayer with proof that the answer is on the way. God wants His people to pray expecting that His answers will appear. Faithless prayers are like a detective coming to a crime scene not expecting to find any evidence; his search will be cursory and fruitless. All of the world's religions encourage people to pray, but only the Word of God requires people to believe what they pray.

This biblical concept to believe what we pray is a radical approach and is the requirement of actually trusting God. Faith is the prerequisite for our prayers to be heard and answered. Jesus said, "I say unto you, whatever things you desire, when you pray, believe that you will receive them, and you shall have them" (Mark 11:24 KJ2000). In order for our prayers to be heard, the Father requires that we maintain an intimate relationship with Him and that we trust Him.

Elijah, who had prophesied the severe famine that was ravaging the land of Israel, heard something that others could not: the sound of heavy rain. After revealing this prophetic word to the king, Elijah took his servant with him to the top of Mount Carmel, bent down to the ground, put his face between his knees and prayed. Then he sent his servant looking toward the sea for the proof of what he had heard. Nothing was evident, but Elijah in faith employed his servant to keep on going back. Tirelessly, the seventh time, the servant finally saw what Elijah was anticipating in prayer. Elijah had forecasted a divine blessing that was on its way. The blessing was, in effect, looking for him. The servant saw a small cloud rising from the sea. The sky grew black, the wind rose, and heavy rain ended the famine (see 1 Kings 18:41–44).

What have you been anticipating? You must pray, building your faith, until you know breakthrough will happen. You have probably seen the acronym *PUSH*: Pray Until Something Happens. Believing in faith will summon your blessing, overflow and surplus. Believing takes the emphasis off prayer itself and puts the emphasis entirely on God. He is our Source. Prayer coupled with faith will bring divine resources. It is all about Him and His faithfulness to answer our prayers. We simply have to believe and expect.

Pray by Faith to Persevere

Scripture does not teach us as believers to rely solely on prayer: It instructs believers to rely on *Him*. Only when we can rely fully on God can we pray fully believing. We are to believe Him first, and then express that belief in prayer. Faith must be resident in our hearts before the prayer comes out of our mouths—even if that faith is so small all it can muster up is a whisper reaching out to God for help. Anticipation is looking forward to something beforehand, foreseeing or being sure it will happen. Our English word *anticipate* comes from a Latin word *anticipare*, which means to "take care of ahead of time" or, literally, "taking into possession beforehand."

It is this original meaning of *anticipation* that I believe the Holy Spirit is bringing to our attention at this time. Anticipation through the eyes of faith is a powerful biblical principle. Anticipation is relentless. We can see in Jesus' parable of the persistent widow how a weak, poverty-stricken individual (the widow) persisted in nagging a powerful, careless and unjust person (the judge) to do justice on her behalf. Jesus focused the parable on the point that we must "always pray and never give up" (Luke 18:1 NLT).

Jesus connected the hearer of the parable—including us today—with the woman and further indicated that God was represented by the careless, unjust judge. A strange combination. We know that Jesus was not saying God is unjust and careless. The point is that one's persistence will eventually pay off, even with an unjust human who possesses limited power. How much more will our persistence pay off with an infinite and just God!

Anticipation is the persistent widow going repeatedly to the courthouse when her requests are ignored. Anticipation is Elijah sending his servant back seven times to see a cloud in the sky. Anticipation is David running toward Goliath with a slingshot and a stone in his hand. Anticipation means taking the necessary steps forward to start the ball rolling. You will find that your anticipation will ignite divine velocity for breakthrough. Anticipation is a powerful spiritual principle but also a practical one. It is expectant action and faith in motion.

I believe that your anticipation and acts of obedience, led and empowered by the Holy Spirit, will bring breakthrough as you take hold of God's promises by faith. The purpose of Jesus' parable about the persistent widow is to encourage us to persevere in our faith against all odds. Only God can bring about justice in a corrupt world. That is why we must pray and never lose heart in our assignments. God can bring miraculous justice in a corrupt world, just as God can bring miraculous healing in a sick world. The widow's persistence alone caused the unjust judge to rule justly. Jesus explained, "Will not God bring about justice for his chosen ones, who cry out to him day and night?" (Luke 18:7). God is the unseen actor waiting for our prayers of faith.

Persevering expectantly is necessary when you are in the process of moving toward your destiny. Power is released when you continue anticipating during difficult times. Hannah is a wonderful example of this in the Bible. Like several other women in Scripture, she was barren. People in ancient Israel believed that a large family was a blessing from God. Infertility, therefore, was a source of humiliation and public shame.

Hannah's husband, Elkanah, had a second wife, Peninnah, and she made things worse by taunting Hannah constantly year after year to make her miserable. Finally Hannah took her pain and poured it out to the Lord in prayer at Shiloh, where Eli was priest. As he watched her pray, he thought she had been drinking. She was praying in her heart; her mouth was moving, but no sound was coming out. She assured Eli that she was not drunk, and he answered, "Go in peace, and may the God of Israel grant you what you have asked of him" (1 Samuel 1:17).

After the family returned from Shiloh to their home at Ramah, Hannah and her husband slept together. Scripture says, "And the Lord remembered her" (1 Samuel 1:19). She became pregnant, had a son and named him Samuel, which means "God hears." But Hannah had made a vow to God that if she bore a son, she would give him back for God's service. Hannah followed through on that promise. She gave the care of her young child over to Eli for training as a priest. God blessed Hannah further for honoring her pledge to Him. Samuel grew up to become the last of Israel's judges, its first prophet and counselor to its first two kings, Saul and David.

Hannah persevered and expected God to come through. Even though God was silent toward her request for a child for many years, she never stopped praying. She had faith that God had the power to help her. After years of praying for the same thing, most of us would have given up. Hannah did not. She was a devout, humble woman, and God finally answered her prayers.

The apostle Paul tells us to "pray without ceasing" (1 Thessalonians 5:17 ESV). We must anticipate God's goodness, never give up, honor our promises to Him and praise Him when the breakthrough comes.

If you want to continue with the daily prayer activations for chapter 2 at this time, please turn to Days 4 through 6, found in part 2 of this book.

PRACTICE JESUS' PRAYER MODEL

Following the template of prayer that Jesus taught His disciples helps us to pray and releases divine breakthrough.

When Jesus had finished praying, one of his disciples said to him, "Lord, teach us to pray, just as John taught his followers to pray."

LUKE 11:1 CEV

God does not want just to teach us how to pray; He wants to teach us how to pray mountain-moving prayers that bring unusual outcomes. He wants to pray unconventional, uncensored, Spirit-led prayers while possessing unflinching faith.

Whether you are a beginner or a seasoned veteran in your spiritual walk with Jesus, you have likely experienced times when your prayers yielded little fruit. Prayer is one of the most misunderstood practices in modern-day religion. I believe that we make prayer into a more complicated art form than it was meant to be. Prayer is simply the reflection of a relationship with God. Once we understand this, it is possible to pray with relentless tenacity, fervency and Holy Spirit passion—and see breakthrough answers.

The Master Teacher

The Father is not looking for perfect prayers. He is looking for people who will talk with Him from a place of intimacy and commitment. We should not focus on mastering the art of prayer; we must master the art of communication. In other words, our focus is to meet with God face-to-face. As we draw close to Him, we find that hearing His voice and feeling His presence become the norm.

The disciples were eyewitnesses of Jesus' miracles, breakthroughs, healings, provisions and divine revelations as a result of His prayer life. They saw that Jesus was immersed in prayer and in the presence of the Father (see Mark 1:35; Luke 6:12; Hebrews 5:7). At some point perhaps they also came to the realization of how little they truly understood prayer. They were stirred with courage and asked Him to teach them (see Luke 11:1–13). They desired to know His prayer secrets so that they, like their Master, might encounter supernatural results. He responded by modeling what praying looks like. He taught by application.

Specifically, Jesus instructed them to access the Father's heart. He enrolled them in the school of prayer expecting them to graduate as prayer warriors and intercessors.

Jesus did not offer His disciples a recycled, legalistic, ritualistic, ineffective and powerless outline to follow. He offered them a breakthrough solution—new language for getting prayers answered. As a teacher, Jesus imparted to them the principle of prayer.

Customizing Jesus' Prayer Life

If someone offered you the key for getting your prayers answered, would you accept that offer? Of course you would. Jesus knew how to commune with His Father through prayer, and the disciples recognized the extraordinary opportunity available for them. This key is available for us as well in the Word of God. As His children we have access to everything we need for our spiritual well-being.

Principally, Jesus showed His followers how to pray faithfully—in other words, how to put their prayers to work by faith. They had to adopt, customize and implement the prayer template, but, ultimately, they were learning how to live in God's presence. This is the key to supernatural prayers that bring supernatural results with the power of God.

A prayer model should not be complicated but complementary! We should not pray conditional prayers that fleece God for something outside of His will, but rather committed prayers that align our hearts with the Lord's direction for our lives. Jesus never failed to speak what He heard the Father speaking and to do what He saw the Father doing (see John 12:49). He was able to imitate on earth what He saw the Father doing in heaven (see Matthew 6:9–10).

While Jesus was on earth, He prayed not only for His disciples but also for all who would follow Him (see John 17:20). He is still praying for us. Jesus is seated at the right hand of God making intercession for you and me daily (see Romans 8:34).

And we can know the very intention of His heart as He prays for us because of the words He gave His disciples when they asked Him how to pray—what we call the Lord's Prayer. This was never meant to be recited as a ritual. Jesus was revealing the key components of prayer, the model for us to apply to our lives. Have you ever noticed how, oftentimes, our prayers start with an anxious series of requests in which we rattle off to the Lord our issues, needs, problems and frustrations—things we want Him to fix? Consequently, we focus more of our attention on being irritated than approaching God for His solution or remedy.

This might be the reason why some people are more frustrated and depressed after they pray than before. In his book *Victorious Praying: Studies in the Lord's Prayer* (Revell, 1993) author Alan Redpath says, "When we have finished our praying we can scarcely bring ourselves to believe that our feeble words can have been heard, or that they can have made a difference in the things concerning which we have been praying. We've said our prayers but we have not prayed."

THE LORD'S PRAYER

There are two versions of the Lord's Prayer. One is found in Matthew 6:9–15. Matthew recorded these words from Jesus' Sermon on the Mount. The second, a slightly shorter version, is recorded by Luke from the time when a disciple came to Jesus and said, "Lord, teach us to pray, just as John taught his disciples" (Luke 11:1 NLT). Rather than delineate prayer principles, Jesus responded to the request for prayer by actually praying.

> "Father, may your name be kept holy. May your Kingdom come soon. Give us each day the food we need, and forgive us our sins, as we forgive those who sin against us. And don't let us yield to temptation."
>
> Luke 11:2–4 NLT

If you do not know how to pray, you can learn. God welcomes us to be like His Son. I believe that everything outlined in Jesus' prayer above should be covered when we pray. Let's think briefly about each key element.

Intimacy with the Father: As followers of Jesus today, we can establish intimacy with the Father that not even the godliest men and women of the Old Testament enjoyed. Not one of them referred to God as Father. Today, we call God *Abba* (Father) through our covenant relationship with Him through Jesus. How does it feel to call God *Father* and see yourself as His child? Natural or awkward?

Honor for the Father: When you pray, do you speak to God as if He is a loved and respected Father, or do you pray as if talking to a master or boss? Holy is God's name! When we talk to God, we should realize that He is not a butler being paid to fetch us what we demand. Or a boss whom we have to try to convince to grant us a little favor. No, we are communicating with the all-powerful Creator who has chosen to reach out to us as a Father who loves His children passionately. That should leave us awestruck and in reverence of His name. How do you posture yourself when you approach God? With respect? With anger or entitlement?

Seeking the Kingdom of God: God's Kingdom coming soon (the ministry of Jesus through the Holy Spirit today and the return of Jesus to earth in the future) should be the first cry of our prayers. Seeking first His Kingdom and His righteousness will bring blessing, favor and increase in every area of our lives (see Matthew 6:33). Ask yourself, "Do I truly desire to see God's Kingdom be established and His will be accomplished in my life?" This is perhaps the key to answered prayer.

Desiring God's will: The prayer recorded by Matthew includes this: "May your will be done on earth, as it is in heaven" (Matthew 6:10 NLT). Jesus said a prayer like this again as He suffered in the Garden of Gethsemane before He was betrayed and crucified: "Not my will, but yours be done" (Luke 22:42). Jesus was always about the Father's business, and Jesus wants that for us, too. God will not answer prayer that is against His will or nature. When we pray for God's will to be done, He has no reason *not* to work according to His will. At the same time, we should ask for wisdom to discern what God's will is for our lives. Are you ready to accept God's will even if it is not yours? Can you pray for discernment to distinguish between God's will and your own?

Requesting daily needs: God is our Source, and Jesus wants us to ask the Father daily to provide for our needs. This is imperative. It helps us to develop reliance on Him, to realize that without Him we can do nothing (see John 15:5). Do you trust God to provide for you each day, or do you tend to keep closer watch on what you have saved in a bank account? Do you rely more on an employer or a government program than you do on God to meet your needs? God is our Provider, and He has daily bread for us—not only the natural bread we eat, but also Jesus, the Bread of Life who feeds our spirits.

Forgiveness: Forgiveness is a big deal because unforgiveness will keep us from the breakthrough God has for us. Forgiveness is mutual. In other words, if you want to be forgiven, then you must learn the principle of forgiving others. If a person sows forgiveness, he or she will reap forgiveness. Is there anything that you need to bring before the Lord with a repentant heart? Is there someone you need to forgive for a wrong against you or someone else?

Deliverance from evil: Temptation itself is not sin. Jesus was tempted but never sinned. Temptation is a doorway opening to sin; prayer will keep us alert to the danger that beckons. One of the best methods for refraining from sin is staying out of situations where we are likely to fall. Avoiding the people and places that tempt us is a lot easier than trying to refrain from wrong when we are in the midst of a compromising situation. In the version of the

Lord's Prayer from the Sermon on the Mount, the words *do not let us yield to temptation* are followed by *rescue us from the evil one.*

The apostle Peter wrote that we must stay alert because we have an enemy who is "looking for someone to devour" (1 Peter 5:8 NLT). Have you ever barged into an unwise situation and asked God to protect you instead of heeding His warning to flee when sin showed itself? Most of us have. When you see evil or sense the presence of the evil one, never stick around! Jude 24 (ESV) tells us that Jesus "is able to keep you from stumbling and to present you blameless before the presence of his glory with great joy." What a wonderful promise!

Communing with the heart of the Father, sure in the knowledge that He hears your prayers and will answer them according to His will, is thrilling. Practicing Jesus' prayer model is the best way to grow in that relationship and maximize your full potential in God.

If you want to continue with the daily prayer activations for chapter 3 at this time, please turn to Days 7 through 9, found in part 2 of this book.

IMPLEMENT FASTING

Consistent prayer while fasting will unlock heavenly
answers, divine blessings and breakthrough.

So we fasted and earnestly prayed that our God would take
care of us, and he heard our prayer.

EZRA 8:23 NLT

D o you have a desire to draw closer to God? Do you feel at
times as though your prayers are bouncing off the walls? Are
you going through a major change in your life? Perhaps you are
experiencing a problem not of your making and are in dire need
of a breakthrough? One key secret I have learned to revolution-
izing my prayer life and experiencing remarkable breakthrough is
implementing a fast.

Throughout the Bible fasting is mentioned more than fifty times.
David prayed and fasted over his ill son (see 2 Samuel 12:16). Anna,
a prophetess who lived to be 84 years old, "never left the temple
but worshiped night and day, fasting and praying" as she awaited

the promised Messiah (Luke 2:37). The prophets and teachers in Antioch fasted and prayed as they commissioned Paul and Barnabas for ministry (see Acts 13:1–3). Even Ahab, Israel's wicked king, fasted so God would not bring judgment on his life (see 1 King 21:27).

What is fasting exactly?

FASTING GETS RESULTS

Fasting is becoming a lost practice. Fasting is simply abstaining from food (or something else) for a period of time in order to redirect your thoughts to God. At its heart it is a special time to enrich your reading of His Word, to meditate, pray and worship. But there is further crucial benefit. If you are facing a difficulty and cannot break through, then fasting is what you need to bring power to your prayers.

God leads people to fast in order to break irresistible strongholds, bad habits, ungodly patterns and unhealthy appetites, and to bring mental clarity, answered prayers, wisdom, direction, physical cleansing, healing and wholeness. Incorporating a fast into our prayer regimens releases the supernatural assistance from the Lord we seek. When I face unexplainable, abrupt resistance or unwarranted blockages in prayer, or I have no answers as to why those things are occurring, I go on a fast.

One time, for instance, I was unemployed for three years and unable to get a job. I prayed often but received no answers. Then I read the Scripture about Daniel fasting and praying and receiving an answer 21 days later. I wanted to test that biblical example out for myself and felt led to go on a three-day fast without food or water.

After finishing my fast on the third day, I received several phone calls and email messages regarding multiple jobs that I had applied for two and three years earlier. Oddly, they all contacted me on the same day to offer me a banking position. The moral of the story is that prayer and fasting worked. Remarkably, what I was praying and waiting for for three years took simply three days of fasting to receive.

I cannot explain the mystery behind it. My point is that I was in desperate need of a breakthrough. The purpose for fasting is not to induce the Lord to respond like a genie in a bottle to grant our every wish. The purpose of any type of fast is primarily to pursue God's heart. All other blessings and benefits are secondary to encountering the Lord Himself. This is what sets apart biblical fasting from the many cultural and religious practices around the world. I believe that prayer is sacred, and fasting is an essential part of praying. God is the Lord of the breakthrough we need.

A Warfare Term

The word *breakthrough* is a commonly used military term. It means that one army will try to weaken its enemy's power by besieging and bombarding it to the point of collapse. A breakthrough then occurs allowing invasion of the enemy's territory.

This concept has a parallel for believers: It describes the kind of warfare we need to employ against our powerful spiritual enemy. Throughout the Word of God we see a consistent pattern: Every significant move of God is preceded by a season of increasing difficulty and discouraging opposition. The devil comes to "wear down the saints" in order to strip and leave us defenseless and susceptible to an onslaught of unexpected attacks (Daniel 7:25).

These are the times when we struggle most for spiritual breakthrough. We need to reach new levels in our walks with God regarding these specific areas that the enemy has targeted. By combining fasting along with prayer, we break through the invisible strongholds that keep us bound. Prayer and fasting are imperative to strengthening our position and causing the enemy's hold to collapse.

This is why you cannot stop praying—because your breakthrough is just up ahead. In fact, if you are not encountering spiritual opposition, it is likely you are not praying targeted prayers in specific areas that the devil is opposing.

Whenever I experience warfare in my family, finances, health, relationships or ministry, I locate strategically in prayer the specific area of opposition and concentrate on breaking through with a particular fast. God instructs what type of fast and how many days are required. Again, we are not fasting to twist God's arm to do anything for us. We are turning our hearts toward the One who can protect and assist us.

Many Christians fail to understand fasting or refuse to do it, but implementing a fast with prayer has the power to shatter attacks from the enemy. Jesus is our example of a lifestyle of fasting and prayer. Remember that at the start of His ministry He fasted for forty days in the wilderness while being tempted by Satan (see Luke 4:2). The more critical the situation, the more appropriate it is that our prayers are joined by fasting.

In Matthew 17 we read that Jesus delivered a boy of an impure spirit. His disciples were previously given authority over unclean spirits (see Matthew 10:1) but were unable to set the boy free.

Later, they asked Jesus why they had failed. He replied, "This kind can come out only by prayer and fasting" (Mark 9:29 ISV).

In this particular case, the unclean spirits were exceptionally violent (see Mark 9:20–22). Jesus was saying that a determined foe must be met with an equally determined faith. Prayer is like an arsenal filled with weapons of spiritual warfare (see Ephesians

6:10–11). Fasting helps us take hold of the resolve we need to use those weapons effectively.

Real spiritual breakthrough is not achieved without prayer. But it is also true that, usually, breakthrough is not achieved by prayer alone—it requires boldness, hard work and courage in the Holy Spirit (see Ephesians 6:12–20). Prevailing prayer, consistency, perseverance and concentration, often engaged in with the help of two or more people (Matthew 18:19), are needed in this warfare. And fasting is a marvelous addition.

Types of Fasting

I love what John Piper says in his book *A Hunger for God* (Crossway, 1997): "Fasting tests where the heart is. And when it reveals that the heart is with God and not the world, a mighty blow is struck against Satan. For then Satan does not have the foothold he would if our heart were in love with earthly things like bread."

Scripturally, fasting is closely associated with a heart of repentance. In the days of Jonah "the people of Nineveh believed God. They called for a fast and put on sackcloth, from the greatest of them to the least of them" (Jonah 3:5 ESV). When we fast, we are seeking the Lord in humility (see Isaiah 58:3–7). Prayer and fasting should not be a mandatory duty or burden but rather a commemoration of God's love, mercy and kindness.

Let's look briefly at four types of fasts.

Regular fast: A regular fast is accomplished by abstaining from all food and liquids, except water. King Jehoshaphat called for a regular fast when his country was faced with enemy invasion. Later the men of Judah praised God because He answered their prayers by defeating all their enemies (see 2 Chronicles 20:1–29). After being exiled, the returning Jews of Jerusalem fasted and prayed, petitioning God for protection on their journey from Babylonian captivity (see Ezra 8:21).

Absolute or full fast: An absolute fast, or full fast, means that no food or water is consumed. Both Moses and Elijah followed this kind of fast supernaturally for forty days consecutively. When Moses met God on the mountaintop to receive the Ten Commandments on tablets of stone, he ate no bread and drank no water (see Deuteronomy 9:9). After Elijah killed the false prophets of Baal on Mount Carmel, infuriating Jezebel, he ran for his life and spent forty days of fasting in the wilderness (see 1 Kings 19:8). When Esther learned of the wicked plot to murder all the Jews in Persia, she and her fellow Jews fasted from food and water for three days before she entered the king's courts to plead for her husband's mercy (see Esther 4:16). Another example of an absolute fast occurred at Paul's conversion when he encountered Jesus on the road to Damascus. "For three days he was blind, and did not eat or drink anything" (Acts 9:9).

Partial fast: Daniel followed a partial fast: "At that time I, Daniel, mourned for three weeks. I ate no choice food; no meat or wine touched my lips; and I used no lotions at all until the three weeks were over" (Daniel 10:2–3). Note that Daniel removed "choice" foods and refrained from using lotions for refreshment. Today, we often refer to a 21-day partial fast as a "Daniel fast," following his example to abstain from desirable foods or pleasurable activities for a short period of time to seek God for supernatural strength, comfort and direction.

Fasting from other substances: In the same way that Daniel chose to fast from lotions, some people fast from things that they enjoy such as entertainment. Some fast from sleep in order to spend more time in prayer and worship. The apostle Paul encouraged married couples to fast from intimacy, but only for a limited period of time and in agreement (see 1 Corinthians 7:5).

How you fast is not important, but it is important to fast in some way. Matthew 6:16 records Jesus as saying *When you fast* not *If you fast*. The purpose of any type of fasting is to give God your intensified focus and receive His perspective. Fasting will enhance all your senses, including your spiritual senses, to hear God's voice about the issue for which you seek His help.

A Secret Weapon!

There is power in prayer and fasting. This combination is vital for believers who want to receive perpetual breakthrough in areas of unseen resistance.

If you are praying for breakthrough and not experiencing it, never lose hope. Opposition precedes breakthrough. A rubber band will give greater resistance the more you stretch it, but the more you stretch it, the closer you get to snapping it. Never give up before your situation snaps and you get your breakthrough. Whether you are contending against your own stubborn sin, salvation for a loved one, financial liberty, healing, the advancing of the Kingdom of God or changing your community or society, you are up against "spiritual forces of evil in the heavenly realms" (Ephesians 6:12). They will oppose you. But through prayer and fasting, you can fight back and see your breakthrough happen.

It is possible to pray without fasting and to fast without praying. But when these two activities are combined and dedicated to God's glory, they reach their full efficiency or potential in our prayer lives. True believers of Christ will fast often and be ready for any warfare. It has been said that prayer is not preparation for warfare—prayer is warfare! Prayer with fasting is one of our most potent secret weapons against the enemy.

If you want to continue with the daily prayer activations for chapter 4 at this time, please turn to Days 10 through 12, found in part 2 of this book.

Cooperate
with God's Timing

Learning how to wait patiently in prayer unleashes
favor, grace and provision from the Lord.

"Take heed, watch and pray; for you do not know when
the time is."

Mark 13:33 nkjv

One difficult thing to hear when you are in a rush is the word
wait. In today's society, everything seems to be moving ex-
peditiously though changing constantly. Often we wish we had
more time, and wasted time is something we cannot get back. Time
waits for no one! Apparently, David felt the pressures of time, as he
prayed expressly, "My times are in your hands" (Psalm 31:15). He
understood that the course of his life was in God's power.

In stating this, David was submitting to God's predestined plan
for his life. Only God determines what our futures hold. We must

cooperate with His perfect timing by faith. It is as we learn the power of waiting patiently in prayer, partnering with Him, that we encounter divine breakthroughs. Through the prophet Jeremiah God said, "'I know the plans I have for you,' declares the Lord, 'plans to prosper you and not to harm you, plans to give you hope and a future'" (Jeremiah 29:11). The Lord has great plans for you. And He promises you a hopeful future.

Time Tested

From the time before we were conceived in our mothers' wombs until the time we take our very last breaths, God's sovereignty is at work fulfilling His eternal purposes in our lives. True, God's timing can test one's faith. But the writer of Hebrews affirms the rewards of patience: "You have need of patience, that, after you have done the will of God, you might receive the promise" (Hebrews 10:36 kj2000).

Habakkuk the prophet needed to learn this. He was growing impatient with the Father's timing: "How long, Lord, must I call for help, but you do not listen?" (Habakkuk 1:2). At some point most of us have said, "Father God, what's taking You so long? Please, hurry up!" We relate to Habakkuk's sentiments. Our prayers reflect our impatience, even petulance.

But the Lord had this response for Habakkuk regarding the promised vision: "The vision awaits its appointed time; it hastens to the end—it will not lie. If it seems slow, wait for it; it will surely come; it will not delay" (Habakkuk 2:3 esv).

Like Habakkuk we must learn to wait on the Lord. So, what does that mean? How do we cooperate with God's timing? Waiting on the Lord is not a passive position. It takes action by faith! It also requires effort, much of which is counterintuitive—particularly to

Millennials, who are used to moving ahead of time. We need to understand that God's timing is perfect, and His ways are perfect (see Psalm 18:30; Galatians 4:4). He is never too early, and He has never been late. He is always on time. He keeps His appointments with His children.

In Due Season

The Bible tells us about another man, Simeon, who was excited about what God had revealed to him and whose faith was tested waiting for its fulfillment (see Luke 2:25–35). As time passed, it might have been difficult for Simeon to believe he would live long enough to see the promised Messiah. Then one day as Simeon was going about his usual activities, the Holy Spirit instructed him to go to the Temple. Simeon may have been busy at that moment, but he decided to stop, listen and obey God's voice.

Upon entering the Temple he saw a young woman standing beside her husband and holding a baby boy in her arms. God's Spirit revealed to Simeon that this baby was in fact the promised Savior.

Immediately, Simeon went to Mary and reached out to hold her newborn son. He held Jesus in his arms, praising God with joy in his heart: "Lord, now you are letting your servant depart in peace, according to your word; for my eyes have seen your salvation" (verses 29–30 ESV). Simeon thanked the Lord not only for sending the Messiah but also for fulfilling His promise to let Simeon see the Child.

At that very moment, while Simeon was praising God and blessing Mary and Joseph, an 84-year-old widow and prophetess named Anna came up to them (see Luke 2:36–39). As a young woman she had been married for seven years, but when her husband died, she served God by fasting and praying, never leaving the Temple. She had a close relationship with God and knew of the Promised Child. Simeon's excitement likely got her attention. As soon as she laid eyes on Jesus, she thanked God for sending the Savior who would take away the sins of the world, and she spoke about Him to all who were looking for His appearing.

Simeon and Anna both saw and believed in God's promised Savior. Gratefully, they praised and thanked God for letting them see the Child. Their patience was tested; however, they possessed relentless faith to wait and cooperate with God's timing. His eternal plan, orchestrated before the foundation of the world, can never be interrupted by human activities. Nor can any event in history put so much as a wrinkle in the fabric of His divine appointments.

We must keep in mind that God is not bound by physical time. God is Spirit and is not limited by the physical laws and dimensions that govern our natural world (see Isaiah 57:15). Moses used a profound but simple analogy to explain the timelessness of God: "A thousand years in your sight are like a day that has just gone by, or like a watch in the night" (Psalm 90:4). The Lord's outlook on time is immensely different from ours (see Psalm 102:12, 24–27). God does not keep time as we do; He exists beyond the sphere of time. God, who is omnipresent, (everywhere at the same time) views all of eternity's past and eternity's future in one moment.

Subsequently, the time that passes on earth is of no consequence from His timeless perspective. One would think, then, that by understanding the sovereignty of our Creator, patience and waiting would come a little more easily. Unfortunately, that is not the case. Our human nature can make waiting for God's perfect timing a difficult thing to do.

Waiting on the Lord

In the hustle and bustle of our hectic lifestyles, we often find it very hard to wait for anything or anyone anymore. As modern technology advances, we have access to almost everything we want when we want it. As a result, we are not only losing our patience but also finding it increasingly difficult to discern the timing of God for our lives. We must learn the principle of watching and praying patiently—like Simeon and Anna. They believed the promise of the coming Messiah and waited for the day that the Lord would fulfill it.

God wants us to learn to be patient because patience is a spiritual fruit (see Galatians 5:22), and we please the Lord when this fruit is at work in our lives. One of the things that I have learned about prayer is that patience reveals our trust level in God's timing. If we are overly anxious to hear from Him, we are probably struggling to trust Him. Yet the Bible says, "Do not be anxious about anything, but in every situation, by prayer and petition, with thanksgiving, present your requests to God" (Philippians 4:6).

The Lord operates solely according to His perfect will and preordained timetable, not ours. Yet as we follow the admonition to "be still before the Lord and wait patiently for him" (Psalm 37:7), we learn that "the Lord is good to those who wait [confidently] for Him" (Lamentations 3:25 AMP). God will give us supernatural strength in prayer: "They who wait for the Lord shall renew their strength; they shall mount up with wings like eagles; they shall run and not be weary; they shall walk and not faint" (Isaiah 40:31 ESV).

Our decision to wait patiently and prayerfully for the perfect timing of God is an indicator of how much we trust Him: "The Lord's unfailing love surrounds the one who trusts in him" (Psalm 32:10). In other words, to wait on God is to know Him and to know His Word. And the best way to know Him is through His Word.

Waiting on God to answer your prayer is cooperating with God's timing—and obeying His Word.

It is not unreasonable that the greater the life crisis, the greater our need for Holy Spirit direction, understanding, deliverance and intervention. But these are just the trials and tribulations that the Lord can use to establish our patience so that our faith is sure, complete and mature (see James 1:3–4). In addition, "we know that in all things God works for the good of those who love him, who have been called according to his purpose" (Roman 8:28).

GOD ANSWERS ON TIME

Are you currently praying and still waiting for God to answer? Waiting is never easy. If, however, you believe that God hears and answers your prayers, then you can have faith that He will answer. His answer will be either yes, no or wait. *Wait* can take a few days, months or years, but God will answer. Ecclesiastes 8:6 assures us that everything that happens in this world to increase our patience happens at the time God chooses.

There have been times when, in growing in God, I have asked myself impatiently, "Is it possible to keep the faith while still waiting on God to answer my prayers?" As I have matured and grown wiser, I have found that it is possible to stay in faith while waiting. I have learned through God's Word about His timing. I have also learned that God will answer our prayers when we least expect Him to. Doubt, unbelief, fear and impatience are obstacles we all must overcome. That is why Scripture says, "When you ask him, be sure that your faith is in God alone. Do not waver, for a person with divided loyalty is as unsettled as a wave of the sea that is blown and tossed by the wind. Such people should not expect to receive anything from the Lord" (James 1:6–7 NLT).

If you are waiting, take inventory of your blessings daily. And remember that no time is ever wasted in God's presence. Though we cannot regain lost time, He can redeem it (Ephesians 5:16). The Lord wants you to turn your time of waiting on Him into a treasure hunt for favor, blessings, grace, love and His divine provision. Rest in God's timing and faithfulness. Psalm 90:12 is a beautiful prayer in this regard: "Teach us to number our days, that we may gain a heart of wisdom." God wants to maximize the time you have here on earth to receive His wisdom and fulfill His purpose. When you make prayer a priority, waiting in faith, patience and assurance, then you will see a greater release of the blessings awaiting you!

If you want to continue with the daily prayer activations for chapter 5 at this time, please turn to Days 13 through 15, found in part 2 of this book.

BE A FRIEND OF GOD

Jesus' friends know His heart and follow His commands,
and that intimacy releases answers to our prayers.

"Abraham believed God, and it was credited to him as righteousness," and he was called God's friend.

JAMES 2:23

Is it possible to befriend God? God is Spirit! What does it take to become God's trusted friend and confidant? There is no mystery behind this phenomenon. It is a biblical fact that God Himself sovereignly called and claimed a man of faith and prayer—Abraham—to be His friend. It is faith that pleases God. From the genesis of time it has been the heart of the Father to have close fellowship with His children.

It is simply mutual intimacy that constitutes a confidential or close companionship between humans and their God. And God, far from making it impossible, unobtainable or mysterious, has pursued that type of friendship and covenant relationship with humankind from the beginning: "Let us make man in our image, after our likeness" (Genesis 1:26 ESV). What defines a friend? It is a person whom one knows and with whom one has a bond of affection. The Greek word for *friend* is *philos*, which means "friend, associate or companion" (Strong's G5384).

THE BASIS OF FRIENDSHIP

Growing up, I often heard the saying, "Birds of a feather flock together." There are certain commonalities among people; throughout the courses of our lives, however, only a select few will meet the criteria of close friends.

Why? One obvious reason is that of agreement. The Bible says, "Can two walk together, except they be agreed?" (Amos 3:3 KJV). Friendship is not meant to be one-sided but rather shared. Ponder that notion for a moment. Our closest friends typically agree with us on most things. Friends think alike. And have a shared commonality. Conflicting minds, dissimilar opinions and opposing preferences do not make for camaraderie. To others we can be on friendly terms— that is, we can have cordial dialogues, enjoying their company—but our closest friends think like us the majority of the time.

Abraham was in continual agreement with God—assenting, obeying, trusting—and this was the basis for their friendship. The apostle James, quoting Genesis 15:6, notes this: "The scripture was fulfilled which says, 'Abraham believed God, and it was reckoned to him as righteousness.'" Then James draws this profound connection: "And he was called the *friend of God*" (James 2:23 RSV, emphasis added).

Notice that in the New Testament James draws attention to the fact that Abraham was known as God's friend in the Old Testament. He uses the term *friend* as the best way to convey the intimacy, trust, love, closeness, loyalty and affection that Abraham and God felt for each other.

Remarkably, it was the all-knowing and all-powerful God who first mentioned the bond of friendship. This was not Abraham's assessment of his relationship with the Lord; nor was it his initial mindset about God. It was a declarative statement that the Lord made about Abraham (see 2 Chronicles 20:7; Isaiah 41:8).

This means that it is, in fact, possible for believers today to become God's friends.

Faith, Prayer and Protection

Abraham was full of faith no matter what—which means he was also full of prayer. Men and women of prayer are considered to be people of faith. Faith keeps you praying and praying keeps you faithful. Abraham, known throughout history as the father of faith, lived in the prayer chamber of God's presence. He practiced the presence of God daily.

Abraham also had favor with God. After his call to leave his people and go where the Lord would show him, Abraham and Sarah traveled and resided temporarily in Gerar. Afraid that King Abimelech would take his life in order to have Sarah, Abraham deceived Abimelech by saying that she was his sister. So the king sent for Sarah and took her.

But the Lord appeared to Abimelech in a dream and warned him not to touch Sarah, informing him that she was Abraham's wife.

Then God said to Abimelech, "Now return the woman to her husband, and he will pray for you, for he is a prophet. Then you will live. But if you don't return her to him, you can be sure that you and all your people will die" (Genesis 20:7 NLT). And the conclusion of the story is that "Abraham prayed to God, and God healed Abimelech and his wife and his maids, so that they bore children. For the LORD had closed fast all the wombs of the household of Abimelech because of Sarah, Abraham's wife" (Genesis 20:17–18 NASB).

God protects His friends. He decided to confront Abimelech in a dream, warning Abimelech not to touch Abraham's wife. Subsequently, Abraham prayed for Abimelech, and he was healed instantly. Also, his wife and maidservants were able to have children. Barrenness was broken off the entire household because of one man's prayers. Abraham's prayers were supernaturally answered because of his friendship with God.

COMPANIONSHIP OF COVENANT

Because of the fellowship between them, Abraham could trust God when He made an extraordinary request: God asked Abraham to sacrifice his son Isaac on an altar. Abraham knew his Friend, however, and knew that He would keep His word to establish a great nation through Isaac. If Isaac were to die, then Abraham believed God would raise him from the dead. He knew that God was not going to renege on His promise.

> By faith Abraham, when God tested him, offered Isaac as a sacrifice. He who had embraced the promises was about to sacrifice his one and only son, even though God had said to him, "It is through Isaac that your offspring will be reckoned." Abraham reasoned that God could even raise the dead, and so in a manner of speaking he did receive Isaac back from death.
>
> Hebrews 11:17–19

This was more than a test. It not only showed Abraham's unfailing trust but also allowed a prophetic glimpse of what the Father

God was going to do at the cross through His own Son. It was not merely God asking Abraham to do something horrendous; it was a revelation about God: that the Lord would not require our lives as payment for sin but would instead provide a living sacrifice. "God so loved the world that he gave his one and only Son" (John 3:16). God's ultimate invitation to fellowship with Him came in sending His Son to pay the price for our sin so that we who believe could be called His children. And He sealed this promise by sending His Holy Spirit as the "guarantee of our inheritance" (Ephesians 1:14 NKJV).

Abraham practiced the presence of God daily. Because of his commitment to a life of prayer, which marked his exceptional faith, God could trust him to foreshadow the consummation of the great plan of redemption. Abraham experienced a personal glimpse into what God was willing to do for our sakes through His Son, Jesus Christ, at the cross.

The Lord refers to Abraham as His friend because he shared God's heart. They were like soldiers who, by suffering together in battle, established a lifelong bond of friendship. Insomuch as this comparative willingness to sacrifice their only sons created a bond between two fathers, Abraham and God were friends.

A Reflection of Intimacy

Although Abraham is the only person in the Bible referred to as the friend of God, other heroes of the faith were friendship material. David befriended God and was known as a "man after [God's] own heart" (Acts 13:22). Daniel was considered "very precious" to the Lord (Daniel 9:23 NLT). Enoch walked so closely with God that one day he disappeared, because God "took him away" (Genesis 5:24). God referred to Moses as "my servant Moses" (Numbers 12:7–8), but Exodus 33:11 says that "the LORD would speak to Moses face to face, as one speaks to a friend." A whole nation can become God's friends. God said to the nation of Israel: "Obey my voice, and I will be your God, and you shall be my people" (Jeremiah 7:23 ESV).

We see, from an incident in the life of Moses, that a friend of God is one who values His presence above all else. Moses had just spent the last forty days alone with God up on Mount Sinai (see Exodus 24:18). While there he had received instructions regarding the Tabernacle and the order of worship, and the two tablets of stone. But while he was gone, the people turned to idolatry, making a golden calf to worship.

At that point God told Moses what was happening—and relayed His intention of destroying such a stiff-necked people. It was only Moses' intercessory prayers that stopped God from destroying the children of Israel in the wilderness (see Exodus 32:1–14).

Our prayer lives reflect our intimacy with God. Friends of God are loyal and covenantal people. Some friendships cannot coexist any more than wickedness and worship can coexist. "Unfaithful people!" exclaimed James. "Don't you know that to be the world's friend means to be God's enemy? If you want to be the world's friend, you make yourself God's enemy" (James 4:4 GNT). God's friends are people whose love for Him transcends the allure of a world system with its concomitant greed, pride and lust (see 1 John 2:15–17).

I do not believe that God the Father or Jesus the Son throws the term *friend* around loosely. With that in mind, read these words of Jesus:

> "I no longer call you servants, because a servant does not know his master's business. Instead, I have called you friends, for everything that I learned from my Father I have made known to you. . . . This is my command: Love each other."
>
> John 15:15, 17

Jesus desires intimacy with those who follow Him, and in return calls them friends.

—— UNBREAKABLE BOND! ——

One of the greatest accolades a believer can receive from the Lord is to be called *His friend*. Jesus wants more than simple obedience from us. He wants a lifelong bond with us such as God and Abraham had through their mutual selfless acts of sacrifice.

I believe we become Jesus' friends when we share in His sufferings. Jesus said, "If any of you wants to be my follower, you must give up your own way, take up your cross daily, and follow me" (Luke 9:23 NLT). His life's mission was to die on the cross to seek and to save the lost. And He instructs us to die to self and our selfish ambitions in order to love others as He did.

If Jesus was willing to pay the ultimate penalty of death to save the lost, then how hard is it for us, with hearts of gratitude and cooperation, to deny ourselves and our selfish desires for the sake of loving others? Being true friends with Jesus means being faithful and loyal when the going gets tough. That is when the tough get going in life.

- ▸ Real friends sacrifice for each other.
- ▸ Real friends support each other.
- ▸ Real friends are reliable and dependable.
- ▸ Real friends are always there.

On the night before His crucifixion, Jesus described the extent of sacrifice that is required for friendship with Him. Jesus said emphatically to His disciples: "Greater love has no man than this, that a man lay down his life for his friends" (John 15:13 RSV). Jesus was true to His statement. He exemplified the ultimate gesture of true friendship and showed what love looks like when He laid down His life for us as the atoning sacrifice for our sins. He paid the price for us that we may live. The daily reminder of Christ's sacrifice will evoke in us the loyalty, dependability and faithfulness found in a friend of God.

If you want to continue with the daily prayer activations for chapter 6 at this time, please turn to Days 16 through 18, found in part 2 of this book.

ACTIVATE ANGELIC HELP

*God sends angels to strengthen believers,
provide protection, fight the enemy, give
messages and guide into His light.*

He will command his angels concerning you to guard you
in all your ways.

PSALM 91:11

Have you ever prayed for something or someone and felt
as though you wasted your time, energy and breath? Or
waited days, weeks or even months, finally to receive an answer
to an urgent matter? Or perhaps wondered why some prayers
take longer than others to get a response from the Lord? This
can be frustrating for anyone who is eager to get an instantaneous reply.

God is not sitting on His throne playing hide-and-seek games
with those He loves, especially those seeking Him diligently for

responses to urgent prayer requests. He longs to answer inquiring minds that desire to know His heart, will and purpose for their lives. We must understand that the Father waits eagerly for us to come to Him so that He can display His love and compassion. The Lord is a faithful Father, who releases divine blessings and favor to those who look forward excitedly to His support (see Isaiah 30:18).

Prayer is not simply something we practice routinely or religiously; it is the art of communication, intimacy and solidarity between humans and their Creator! And one way God responds to this touching of hearts is to send angels on our behalf. He will activate and assign angels in answer to our prayers, to help us receive supernatural breakthrough.

INVISIBLE FRIENDS TO THE RESCUE

Angels or "ministering spirits" (Hebrews 1:14) are assigned to serve the purposes of God in our lives—whatever form that service might take. The Greek word *minister* is *diakoneó*, meaning "to wait at a table, aid or to serve" (Strong's G1247). The Bible gives us a great deal of evidence of their activity and visitations.

Angels appeared to Jacob in a vision going up and down a ladder to heaven (see Genesis 28:12). An angel fed Elijah a cake of bread and gave him water (see 1 Kings 19:5–7). While Daniel was in the lions' den, God sent an angel to his rescue to shut the mouth of the lions (see Daniel 6:22).

God sent an angel with prophetic messages to Mary, the mother of Jesus (see Luke 1:28). He sent an angel in dreams to warn Joseph of imminent danger concerning the Child (see Matthew 2:13).

An angel from heaven encouraged and strengthened Jesus in the Garden of Gethsemane (see Luke 22:43). Following the temptations in the wilderness, the devil left Jesus and "angels came and ministered unto him" (Matthew 4:11 KJV).

When Peter and other apostles were imprisoned for preaching about Jesus, God sent an angel to rescue them so they could continue to share the Good News with others: "During the night an angel of the Lord opened the prison doors and brought them out, and said, 'Go and stand in the temple and speak to the people all the words of this Life'" (Acts 5:19–20, 29 ESV).

An angel was sent to rescue Peter from prison another time as well:

> The very night [before Herod was to bring him to trial], Peter was sleeping between two soldiers, bound with two chains. And the guards before the door were securing the prison. And suddenly an angel of the Lord approached him, and a light shone in the prison. He struck Peter on the side and woke him up, saying, "Rise up, quickly." And the chains fell off his hands.
>
> Acts 12:6–11 MEV

Angels stand ready to do whatever God commands them to do. They carry provision from His storehouse. They are His reapers and gatherers. They bind demonic powers that restrict us from walking in the purposes of God. They bring deliverance. They provide protection and strength. God also uses them as His healing agents.

God uses our invisible friends to protect and complete His purposes in all our lives. You are surrounded by a host of angelic warriors and guardians whether you see them or not: They are encamped around the believer (see Psalm 34:7). They will come to your rescue, doing God's will and obeying His Word (see Psalm 91:11; 103:20).

——— Unseen Warfare ———

Why is angelic help so much a part of our lives? Because there is a battle occurring in the unseen realm. God opened the spiritual eyes of Elisha's servant to see an angelic army surrounding them on a hill with horses and chariots of fire ready to go to war for them (see 2 Kings 6:16–17). God opened Daniel's spiritual sight by unveiling a war in the angelic realm. The angel Gabriel explained to Daniel that God had sent the archangel Michael, a warring angel, to assist him in battle against the spiritual prince of the kingdom of Persia (see Daniel 10:13–14).

I love what Hebrews 1:14 (AMP) states about angels called to God's people: "Are not all the angels ministering spirits sent out [by God] to serve (accompany, protect) those who will inherit salvation?" God is not using chocolate soldiers that will melt under the heated pressure of the devil.

Unseen warfare and opposition are always at work trying to hinder our answers from being manifested. The devil knows that angels are on assignment to bring our breakthroughs. He was formerly an angel of light in heaven called Lucifer. Now, fallen, he will fight those who will pray.

God wants us to become relentless prayer warriors of Christ who will showcase resilience in the eyes of adversity and pray until something happens. We will face opposition that tries to resist His purposes from coming forth in our lives. But I have learned that opposition is an opportunity that God uses to deliver His promises to us.

In other words, what the enemy intends for our evil or demise, God will use for our good. He will turn the tables on the devil (see Genesis 50:20). Furthermore, when there is intense resistance in the natural all around you, this is an indication of the battle going on in the spiritual—and it is then that God deploys angelic assistance for you. God will send angels to rescue you in times of need.

Getting Heaven's Attention

The Lord will not have His people oblivious to the enemy's schemes (see 2 Corinthians. 2:11). That is why it is imperative never to stop praying—and to ask the Lord to send angelic help. In prayer is where the plans of the enemy are exposed. Remember this truth from Scripture: The prayers of the righteous are "powerful and effective" (James 5:16).

Think again of Daniel. Daniel did not stop praying because his prayer was not answered. He practiced the art and principle of prayer that unlocks angelic involvement and releases heavenly answers. He persevered in prayer and fasting for 21 days until his answer broke through. He knew how to get heaven's attention to respond to his pleas. In a time of national crisis his fervent prayers brought solutions.

Your breakthrough answers are hanging in the balance between heaven and earth. Angels will deliver them to you as you partner with God to pray without ceasing (see 1 Thessalonians 5:17). Praying without ceasing means not stopping, which implies constancy (see Colossians 4:2) and perseverance (see Luke 18:1; Romans 12:12; Ephesians 6:18).

Angelic Partnership

I want to encourage you that your breakthrough blessing is on the way. There are reasons sometimes beyond human understanding why the Lord takes His time in answering our prayers. The key point is not to stop praying until you experience the promises of God made manifest through His angelic services. When you pray according to His will, God dispatches His angels in response to your prayers.

It will take spiritual discipline and patience to see supernatural breakthrough happening in your life and in the lives of others you are praying for. Be confident that your prayers are heard! "If anyone is a worshiper of God and does his will, God listens to him" (John 9:31 ESV). Pray with faith and expectation that our Father who is God in heaven will respond to those who believe He exists and reward those who diligently seek Him (see Hebrews 11:6).

In addition "this is the confidence that we have in Him, that if we ask anything according to His will, He hears us. And if we know that He hears us, whatever we ask, we know that we have the petitions that we have asked of Him" (1 John 5:14–15 NKJV). The angels are waiting for us to make the first act of faith that will initiate God's command to answer our prayers and bring the breakthrough we are waiting for.

Waiting to Be Commissioned

We can be confident that the Lord hears the prayers of His children. He responds quickly to our cry (Psalm 34:17). Angels usher in the presence of God and declare His divine purpose to the one who prays.

We should pray heaven's agenda actively, cultivating worshipful hearts, in order to encounter powerful results. It is an amazing dynamic, a living cycle. In response to our prayers, God commissions angelic servants to guard, heal, deliver and strengthen us, to execute His judgments, to gather, to reap and to do whatever else He desires them to do for us. Then as our prayers are answered,

He sends angels to help us understand what to pray for next—and the cycle repeats.

Angels are prophetic watchers (see Daniel 4:13–17). They look into the affairs of humans. They mentor and coach us in watchful praying and alertness. They alarm us when they spot something. They also advise each other, and they go into warfare whenever the need arises. Angels are closely engaged in our spiritual conflicts. We cannot fight against the devil without them. Without their assistance we cannot carry out or fulfill our assignments as commanders of prayer. Paul wrote, "Do not be anxious about anything, but in every situation, by prayer and petition, with thanksgiving, present your requests to God" (Philippians 4:6).

I believe our angels are unemployed at times because we have stopped praying. Prayer is spiritual life support for the believer. Angels are assigned to our prayers! God will not deploy them until we employ prayer. Next time you think about praying for something or someone, remember you have more with you than against you ready to bring your prayers to pass. Arise in prayer! Activate God's ministering angels who are standing guard to help you break through.

If you want to continue with the daily prayer activations for chapter 7 at this time, please turn to Days 19 through 21, found in part 2 of this book.

FORGIVE

Praying for those who have wronged you will unlock a
wealth of blessings and supernatural breakthroughs.

"And when you stand praying, if you hold anything against
anyone, forgive them, so that your Father in heaven may
forgive you your sins."

MARK 11:25

A dominating theme throughout the Bible that most Christians would rather overlook or ignore, and seem rarely to discuss, is forgiveness. But at the same time, it is not uncommon for believers to have many questions about it. To forgive someone is more than just saying, "I forgive you." This is an action word.

One may ask, What does forgiveness have to do with prayer? Well, it has everything to do with prayer. Also, it has everything to do with why most of our prayers are not answered. Forgiveness should not be viewed as a taboo topic among those who walk in the love of Christ. Forgiveness is the ultimate reason why God the Father sent His Son, Jesus, to seek and save the lost.

The Bible does not define *forgiveness* but rather presents a plethora of examples of people who forgave. The forgiveness of God—the forgiving nature of God—is the greatest example. I love what Oswald Chambers says in his classic *My Utmost for His Highest*: "Forgiveness is the divine miracle of grace." Although the following passage of Scripture does not use the word *forgive*, it describes perfectly God's idea of what unconditional love looks like through His eyes of compassion:

> The LORD is compassionate and gracious, slow to anger, abounding in love. He will not always accuse, nor will he harbor his anger forever; he does not treat us as our sins deserve or repay us according to our iniquities. For as high as the heavens are above the earth, so great is his love for those who fear him; as far as the east is from the west, so far has he removed our transgressions from us.
>
> Psalm 103:8–12

THE POWER TO FORGIVE

Throughout the Word of God we must note that forgiveness functions in the realm of sin. What is sin? The dictionary describes it as "an immoral act considered to be a transgression against divine law, an act regarded as a serious or regrettable fault, offense or omission." Sin is an offense against God or another person. Many passages of Scripture that contain the word *forgive* or *forgiveness* also mention the word *sin*.

The power of prayer is effective when the power of forgiveness is active. Job 42:7–8, for instance, says this:

After the Lord had said these things to Job, he said to Eliphaz the Temanite, "I am angry with you and your two friends, because you have not spoken the truth about me, as my servant Job has. So now take seven bulls and seven rams and go to my servant Job and sacrifice a burnt offering for yourselves. My servant Job will pray for you, and I will accept his prayer and not deal with you according to your folly."

God allowed Job to intercede for his foolish friends. God told them that if they wanted to be forgiven and be received back into His good graces, they could offer sacrifices—but only if Job prayed for them. What a thought-provoking lesson about prayer and intercession! God was going to judge Job's three friends harshly unless Job prayed for them. This is the power of prayer: It can block God's judgment and bring restoration. The sovereign God put the outcome of three men's lives in the hands of one man's intercession.

Can you see the significance of prayer when we forgive and intercede for others? Can you imagine the consequences if Job had decided not to pray and forgive? Can you picture the lives lost if Job had chosen to hold a grudge instead? How destitute our lives and the lives of those we love will be if we undermine the effectiveness of prayer and forgiveness! God pardoned and forgave Job's friends because of his prayers—not theirs.

Prayer That Pardons

Think about it. As we walk in forgiveness, we have the power through intercessory prayer to exonerate others spiritually for the wrongs they have committed against us. By the same token, however, if we choose not to forgive, we are hindering our own spiritual freedom. Any time we harbor unforgiveness in our hearts, chances are pretty good that our prayers are answered only because God has accepted someone else's intercession on our behalf. The choice to forgive gives us the power to release to God those who committed wrongful acts against us, as well as lift judgment off us that comes from walking in unforgiveness.

I can imagine Job's prayer sounding something like this: "O God, here are my three hardheaded, rebellious and foolish friends. You forgave me; please forgive them and bless them, because they know not the ramifications of what they have done. I forgive them, Lord!" The Lord heard Job's prayer and accepted it, and his friends were forgiven. What is so powerful about prayer and forgiveness is that the Bible says this: "After Job had prayed for his friends, the LORD restored his fortunes and gave him twice as much as he had before" (Job 42:10).

What an amazing lesson that Job interceded for them without a vestige of resentment or any attempt to get even! He simply lifted them up before the Lord. God honored Job's prayer, forgave his friends and restored them to His grace.

Then God gave Job double for his trouble. Could it be possible that our increase, divine blessings and supernatural breakthroughs are tied up in our forgiving and praying for others? Apparently, they were for Job and could be for us as well.

Our supernatural breakthroughs are contingent upon the way we love, pray for and forgive others. The act of forgiving is not easy. Our natural response is to recoil in a defensive mode when we have been hurt. Subsequently, we do not naturally feel grace, understanding and mercy when we have been violated. But what does the Bible teach us about forgiveness? Is it an emotional state of mind? Or is it rather a conscious decision? I believe that forgiveness is a choice we all have to make in life. It is a move of the will, inspired by the Holy Spirit.

FORGIVENESS: THE WHY AND HOW

The Word of God admonishes us to forgive for one simple reason: The Lord forgave us. "Bear with each other and forgive one another if any of you has a grievance against someone. Forgive as the Lord forgave you" (Colossians 3:13). Jesus said, "Forgive, and you will be forgiven" (Luke 6:37). Christ also repeats this to the disciples soon after praying the Lord's Prayer: "If you forgive other people when they sin against you, your heavenly Father will also forgive you" (Matthew 6:14).

We forgive because the Bible says to. As children of God it is our moral duty to do so out of obedience.

Okay, you might say. But *how* do we forgive someone when we are not ready to? Or do not feel like it? Or think it is impossible? We forgive by faith! It is possible to forgive when the love of Christ is working in us by the Holy Spirit.

Since forgiveness goes against our nature, we must forgive by faith whether we feel like it or not. The sooner we forgive, the better we will be able to move on with our lives successfully. We trust God's process to finish the work in us by the Holy Spirit, so that our forgiveness will be complete. Our faith assures us of God's promise to help us demonstrate this Christlike character.

People who have been maligned, violated and injured tend to own the offenses and harbor resentment in their hearts. The enemy knows that if unforgiveness takes root in the lives of believers, then it becomes a legal right for him to block, hinder and highjack their blessings. As we take our hurts to prayer, God reveals the dark areas of our souls so we can find resolution regarding those who have offended us, as well as those we have offended. Forgiveness obliterates the demonic strongholds that keep God's people hostage to past offenses.

There are times in prayer when I ask God to do something for me, and He brings to my attention an unrepented sin, wrongful act or unresolved issue toward someone. Unless I seek His heart about resolving the offense, I am holding up my own, or someone else's, breakthrough blessings.

FORGIVE AND FORGET?

How will you know if you have truly forgiven? There is a phrase we often hear: "Forgive and forget." This, however, is misleading. It is wrong to expect an individual who has been abused all of a sudden to have sanctified amnesia.

Realistically, if something traumatic happened in our lives, we will always remember that experience. On the other hand, we can make a conscious decision to forgive and not demand recompense or even acknowledgment from the offender. In *Forgive and Forget* (Harper, 1984), Lewis B. Smedes states profoundly: "When you release the wrongdoer from the wrong, you cut a malignant tumor out of your inner life. You set a prisoner free, but you discover that the real prisoner was yourself."

The Old Testament prophet Jeremiah spoke these words from God: "I will forgive their wickedness, and I will never again remember their sins" (Jeremiah 31:34 NLT). This means that God chooses not to hold our sins against us when we genuinely repent. Likewise, when we forgive, we expunge the other from what has been done against us.

I believe that *forgive* and *forget* are two terms that express the optimal result of dealing with our hurts. If we have truly forgiven someone, then we will not constantly hold that offense against the wrongdoer or apply the sins of the past to any future altercations. The Bibles says that love "keeps no record of wrongs"

(1 Corinthians 13:5). To forget, biblically speaking, is deciding not to act on sins against us even though we may remember the unfortunate circumstances. Our forgiveness is complete when we encounter freedom and peace about the hurtful past.

Total forgiveness is a core message throughout the Gospel. Jesus forgives us totally, and He expects no less from us in our dealings with our fellow human beings. God wants us, in prayer, to root out the hidden and hardened places where resentment resides. We are the ones who suffer the most when we refuse to exercise the power of forgiveness. When we *do* forgive, God liberates our hearts from the toxic imprisonment of anger and bitterness.

Forgiveness is not an overnight process. Many times we want justice concerning the ones we need to forgive. It takes time to be able to pray for those who hurt us, but in the meantime we can ask God to deal with the unfairness. We can trust God to judge the lives of the offenders and make things right. Then we can leave those prayers and *them* at the altar so God can take care of it.

Never Stop Forgiving

Peter came to Jesus asking, "'Lord, how often shall my brother sin against me, and I forgive him? Up to seven times?' Jesus said to him, 'I do not say to you, up to seven times, but up to seventy times seven'" (Matthew 18:21–22 NKJV). Clearly, Jesus understood that forgiveness is not easy and is not a onetime act or decision.

Essentially, He was saying, "Keep on forgiving until you encounter the liberating power of forgiveness." For some individuals forgiveness may take a lifetime to accomplish, but it is imperative.

The secret of forgiveness is found in the power of prayer! Prayer is one of the most effective ways to tear down the barriers erected in our hearts. Jesus said, "Pray for those who persecute you! In that

way, you will be acting as true children of your Father in heaven"
(Matthew 5:44–45 NLT). When you pray for someone you need to
forgive, you demonstrate that you are a child of God.

Also, prayer will assist you in hearing the voice of God and sens-
ing His heart to forgive. As you pray, you begin to see through the
lens God uses to see that person—you start to see a person who
is precious to Him. You also see yourself in a new light—a person
just as guilty of sin and failure whom Jesus has redeemed.

If God does not withhold His forgiveness from us, how can we
withhold forgiveness from another? And why should we stay in the
torment? Unforgiveness is lethal; it works *against us*. Forgiveness
is our greatest weapon against self-inflicted pain.

Although it is normal for believers to feel righteous anger against
injustice and sin, it is not in our authority to judge or condemn
another. Jesus said, "Do not judge, and you will not be judged.
Do not condemn, and you will not be condemned. Forgive, and
you will be forgiven" (Luke 6:37). When you forgive, it empowers
everyone involved to recognize and receive God's grace.

*If you want to continue with the daily prayer acti-
vations for chapter 8 at this time, please turn to
Days 22 through 24, found in part 2 of this book.*

UNLEASH
CHAIN-BREAKING PRAISE

Partnering with heaven through praise creates space
for His divine blessings to be released over our lives.

> And at midnight Paul and Silas prayed, and sang praises
> unto God: and the prisoners heard them.
>
> ACTS 16:25 KJV

Something incredibly powerful happens when you pray. The enemy knows this, and he will use anything from his limited arsenal to keep you from praying. He understands that if he can distract you or create a situation that changes your course of action and attitude toward prayer, he has won half the battle.

I say "half the battle" because prayer alone is not enough to overcome the strategies of the enemy against you. Praise provides the extra blow that causes him to retreat. Praising in prayer is your strongest weapon!

Whenever I am facing difficulties or depression, or feel over-whelmed by life, I have learned to use "praise power," guided by the Holy Spirit, to receive my breakthrough. Prayer and praise are like a double-edged battle-ax against the enemy of your purpose. Whenever you are pushed into a corner of life and feeling troubled, oppressed or defeated, just use your weapon of praise. It is in your mouth!

Psalm 18:3 says, "I called to the LORD, who is worthy of praise, and I have been saved from my enemies." When we call on the Lord in prayer and release praises to Him, He then rescues us from the enemy's snares. Satan and the powers of darkness are no match for a believer who is genuinely offering up praise, honor and thanksgiving unto God in anticipation of personal deliverance.

The Right Approach

What is praise? It begins with the way we come into God's pres-ence: There is a divine protocol. Anyone who appears before a king, judge, president or prime minister approaches with honor and respect, acknowledging the seat of authority. It is the same when we come before God in prayer. We enter the King's court with hearts of thanksgiving and praise regardless of how we might feel at the moment.

> Shout joyfully to the LORD, all the earth. Serve the LORD with glad-ness; come before Him with joyful singing. Know that the LORD Himself is God; it is He who has made us, and not we ourselves; we are His people and the sheep of His pasture. Enter His gates with thanksgiving and His courts with praise. Give thanks to Him, bless His name. For the LORD is good; His lovingkindness is everlasting and His faithfulness to all generations.
>
> Psalm 100 NASB

There are seven Hebrew words translated *praise*. One is *yadah*, meaning "give thanks" (Strong's H3034). A second is *zamar*, which means "sing praise" (Strong's H2167). A third is the word *halal* (the root of *hallelujah*), meaning "to honor or commend" (Strong's H1984). Every definition of *praise* affirms the act of offering up reverence, honor and thanksgiving to the One who is worthy.

Prayer places you into position to communicate more closely with God; praise opens the door and ushers you in. God inhabits the praises of His people (Psalm 22:3). He lives in our praise. He searches for it.

Did you realize that when God sees His children coming in prayer with praise in their mouths, He creates a space for His divine blessings to be released over their lives? God will not restrain His favor, goodness and provision. Praise opens the gateway of blessing. "Blessed be the God and Father of our Lord Jesus Christ, who has blessed us with all spiritual blessings in heavenly places in Christ" (Ephesians 1:3 KJ2000). Partnering with heaven through prayer and praise creates a supernatural atmosphere for liberty, healing, salvation and deliverance to take place.

— PRAISE POWER —

God does not want us to pray general prayers; He wants us to become "generals" in prayer! It is in prayer that we hear God's voice giving us instructions for the situations we are facing. We see this in the way He led King Jehoshaphat in battle, a story told in 2 Chronicles 20. The only weapon King Jehoshaphat used was songs of praise! After praying to God for help, the king gave a directive to organize a choir. Men went out at the head of the army singing and praising the Lord. As three opposing nations rose against them, the people of God believed that they would be victorious.

As the choir began to sing, God sent a surprise attack against the armies of Ammon, Moab and Mount Seir, who were invading Judah—and they were suddenly defeated. In fact, the outcome of the battle against the enemy was devastating. The Lord in His sovereignty did something unprecedented and unpredictable: He sent an ambush, a sneak attack. The enemy was so confused by the shouting and praising that they started fighting and killing one another.

They all died in battle, and the people of Judah never even had to lift their swords. The only thing they lifted was a voice of praise, and God hit the enemy hard with a mighty arm (see Psalm 89:13; 98:1; 118:15–16). They did not have to fight because the finger of God brought them victory and deliverance.

Whether you can sing or not, praise causes the Father to come down to see about His child. Never allow the enemy to bring confusion, doubt, stress or oppression into your life. Fight back in prayer with praise, and you will change the whole narrative of the spiritual battle. God does not want us moping around defeated. God desires for us to be victorious believers in Christ.

If ever you cannot muster enough strength in prayer, just lift your voice in thanksgiving, and watch God bring breakthrough, deliverance, freedom and healing into your life. Let praise become your battle cry of freedom.

Spiritual Resistance

God will ambush not only the enemies you can see but also the invisible opposition against you in the spiritual realm.

Colossians 4:2 (NASB) is a key verse in this regard: "Devote yourselves to prayer, keeping alert in it with an attitude of thanksgiving." God wants to change our attitudes about praying and praising Him. If the enemy can turn our attention to the problem instead of the

Problem Solver—Christ Jesus—then he has the advantage. If the enemy can cause us to become fearful, timid or anxious, then he has control.

Philippians 4:6 (NASB) tells us how to respond: "Be anxious for nothing, but in everything by prayer and supplication with thanksgiving let your requests be made known to God." You must not allow the enemy to rob you of what is rightfully and legally yours as a child of God. The agenda of hell is revealed and darkness is pushed back when you pray with thanksgiving.

I am reminded of a story in the Bible of two men of God who were on their way to prayer but were met with demonic resistance.

> Now it happened, as we went to prayer, that a certain slave girl possessed with a spirit of divination met us, who brought her masters much profit by fortune-telling. This girl followed Paul and us, and cried out, saying, "These men are the servants of the Most High God, who proclaim to us the way of salvation." And this she did for many days. But Paul, greatly annoyed, turned and said to the spirit, "I command you in the name of Jesus Christ to come out of her." And he came out that very hour.
>
> Acts 16:16–18 NKJV

We can see that these men were intentional about what they were on their way to do, and that was to pray. Whether you know it or not, invisible forces will try to restrict and prevent you from getting into the presence of God in prayer. This possessed girl was a fortune-teller who was making money for her master. She was able to recognize something authentic about them.

Furthermore, she followed them for days shouting their true spiritual identity as men of the Most High God. Paul, being greatly irritated while discerning the spirit of divination at work in her, spoke to the spirit to come out in Jesus' name, and it came out. Paul exhibited Holy Spirit power and boldness as a result of a dedicated prayer life. As we pray, the Holy Spirit will give us power, wisdom and boldness to address pestering things that come against us when we are in pursuit of God's presence.

The owners of the slave girl were furious that their business was shut down. They dragged Paul and Silas before the magistrates, who ordered them to be beaten severely and locked in prison. While in jail, Paul and Silas did not dwell on their present condition. They shifted their focus and attitude onto something beyond themselves. The answer for these two men, supernatural release, came because of their prayer and songs of praise, which brought sudden, earth-shaking transformation.

Midnight Praise Break

A miracle was about to happen for Paul and Silas.

> About midnight Paul and Silas were praying and singing hymns to God, and the prisoners were listening to them, and suddenly there was a great earthquake, so that the foundations of the prison were shaken. And immediately all the doors were opened, and everyone's bonds were unfastened.

> Acts 16:25–26 esv

The Lord will shake things up through your praise! When Paul and Silas partnered prayer with praise at midnight, God sent an earthquake to loosen their chains—and the chains of the other prisoners as well. Praise will break every chain in your life—as well as those binding the lives of people you are praying for. The entire prison experienced deliverance, freedom, salvation—even suicide prevention.

Your darkest moment is when you should give God your brightest praise. Paul and Silas took full advantage of brutal treatment to bring mass deliverance to those in prison. What the enemy meant for evil God turned around for good. The two men waited for the right time—midnight—while the prison cells were quiet to pray and sing praises. They lifted up their voices loud and clear, and God responded by shaking the foundations and setting everyone free.

Praise Alw.

We have to learn how to praise God in t. ... seen resistance and unexpected persecution. First Thes. 5:16–18 tells us to "rejoice always, pray continually, give th. ll circumstances; for this is God's will for you in Christ Jes.

This means praising God in advance before you see a of victory. In fact, the real test for the believer is praising Go n it looks as though He is not going to do anything for you This is why Job was commended for not cursing God after lo his health and all of his fortune.

Can you praise God in the midst of your current storm?

Consider this: You can weather the storm with your praise! King David said it empathically: "I will bless the Lord at all times; his praise shall continually be in my mouth. . . . O magnify the Lord with me, and let us exalt his name together" (Psalm 34:1, 3 rsv). David knew the power of praise that brought divine healing and heavenly benefits (see Psalm 103:1–3).

Praise should always be in our mouths. Why? Because it will confuse and dwarf the enemy's plans every time. It will create a supernatural crack in any wall standing between you and your breakthrough. It will unleash heaven on earth in your life.

If you want to continue with the daily prayer activations for chapter 9 at this time, please turn to Days 25 through 27, found in part 2 of this book.

PARTNER WITH THE
HOLY SPIRIT AND OTHERS

Jesus sent the Holy Spirit to be our helper.
Partnering with Him and a few others
releases supernatural breakthrough.

"The Helper, the Holy Spirit, whom the Father will send in my name, will teach you everything and make you remember all that I have told you."

JOHN 14:26 GNT

Waiting on God for an answer to prayer answer is hard. Waiting on Him for a very long time is even harder. Waiting on Him all by yourself for a very long time is the hardest. It is difficult to stand while battling things alone. This does not have to be. God desires for us to partner with the Holy Spirit and others in prayer.

The Bible says:

> Two people are better off than one, for they can help each other
> succeed. If one person falls, the other can reach out and help. But
> someone who falls alone is in real trouble. . . . A person standing
> alone can be attacked and defeated, but two can stand back-to-back
> and conquer. Three are even better, for a triple-braided cord is not
> easily broken.
>
> Ecclesiastes 4:9–10, 12 NLT

I believe two primary things we must learn when it comes to
prayer are how to hear from the Lord and how to share with others
what God has given us to share. Sometimes our breakthroughs to
answered prayer come as a result of other believers fighting on our
behalf. You are not alone!

— Prayer Partners —

Everything you receive from the Father in answer to prayer will
happen according to His will for your life (see Matthew 7:7). Remember: Your prayers are answered when you pray in agreement
with God's will, and only then. If someone joins you in the prayers
that are on God's heart, it creates a Holy Spirit partnership that I
call a "prayer agreement."

Jesus described this in Matthew 18:19–20 (KJV): "I say unto you,
That if two of you shall agree on earth as touching any thing that they
shall ask, it shall be done for them of my Father which is in heaven.
For where two or three are gathered together in my name, there am
I in the midst of them." Prayer partners are other believers who pray
in total agreement with you and for you. In addition, they pray as
the Holy Spirit directs. This builds your prayer power. The enemy

knows the strength of agreement and of godly covenants and assigns invisible forces to block your prayers. It is vital to have those who will stand in agreement in prayer with you—who have your back.

Moreover, the Holy Spirit is the secret weapon in prayer against the enemy's plots. Teaming with the Holy Spirit is necessary because oftentimes we do not know what to pray for or we pray amiss for something that is not God's will (see James 4:3). I love what Romans 8:26 (ESV) says: "The Spirit helps us in our weakness. For we do not know what to pray for as we ought, but the Spirit himself intercedes for us with groanings too deep for words."

The Father in heaven wants you first to come into total agreement with His eternal will and purpose regarding your prayer concerns. Secondly, you partner with other like-minded, passionate and purposeful believers in faith to "touch and agree" on God's will for you here on earth. Lastly, you ask for the Holy Spirit's empowerment to assist and anoint you to fulfill God's perfect will in Jesus' name. God hears us when we pray alone, but calling on the Holy Spirit's help with prayer partners gets heavenly attention and answers! The Father not only delights in hearing our prayers but loves to answer them as well (see Hebrews 11:6).

A popular African proverb says, "It takes a village to raise a child." Ponder the notion that it takes a whole community to raise one child. The success or failure of a church, city or nation does not fall on one person but on everyone—especially the leadership! God desires to establish cultures of prayer that bring supernatural benefits to everyone involved.

Intercessory Prayer of Breakthrough

Here is a prime example, a story told in Acts 12:1–18. When Peter was arrested and facing trial before King Herod, the New Testament

Church had what I call an all-night prayer shut-in to activate the power of agreement and intercession.

The believers had gotten word that Peter was on death row. They decided to take matters into their own hands by going to God in prayer, an effort that required much physical and spiritual strength.

Meanwhile, as this body of believers was standing in the gap for Peter, an angel came suddenly, woke him up, released his handcuffs and told him to get dressed and get out of there. Peter thought he was dreaming. He did not realize that an angel was assisting him in his release. He walked past the guards, entered through the iron-gate leading to the city and was then suddenly left by the angel at an intersection. Apparently, Peter understood at that point that God had sent angelic assistance to rescue him from Herod's vicious plans.

When Peter arrived at John Mark's mother's house—her name was Mary—it was packed with praying friends. They were overwhelmed when they saw him.

And back at the jail, daybreak brought an uproar. Peter was nowhere to be found. The corporate and relentless intercession by the saints had orchestrated his release. When believers of faith decide to come together to pray for each other, the impossible becomes possible!

Can you picture your friends gathering together in prayer to protest the enemy's plans for you? Are you willing to join others to contend for their breakthroughs? Partnering with other believers and the Holy Spirit can cause God to dispatch supernatural reinforcements and change the narrative of the enemy's plots.

The power of corporate prayer is vital in our Christian walks. Learning how to stand in the gap with others will bring mutual and long-lasting benefits. And, on the other hand, when we fail to take this stance, we can thwart the good that God wants to do for us. Ezekiel the prophet warned God's people of impending danger, but they refused to join his call to prayer. So God said, "I sought for a man among them who would make a wall, and stand in the gap before Me on behalf of the land, that I should not destroy it; but I found no one" (Ezekiel 22:30 NKJV).

The Holy Spirit will empower us as we stand ready to battle in spirit even if our flesh is weak (see Matthew 26:41).

Holy Spirit Partnership

Effective praying must be accomplished with the assistance and power of the Holy Spirit. Acts 4:31 (ESV) says: "And when they had prayed, the place in which they were gathered together was shaken, and they were all filled with the Holy Spirit and continued to speak the word of God with boldness."

Praying with Holy Spirit empowerment will shake things up and bring courage, boldness and strength: "Dear friends, [build] yourselves up in your most holy faith and [pray] in the Holy Spirit" (Jude 20); "[pray] at all times in the Spirit, with all prayer and supplication. To that end, keep alert with all perseverance, making supplication for all the saints" (Ephesians 6:18 ESV).

Praying at all times in the Spirit is accomplished when we depend solely, intellectually and emotionally upon the Spirit of God to help us pray to God the Father through His Son, Jesus Christ. When believers pray in agreement and in accordance with God's Spirit, we can effectively pray God's will and be confident He will answer our petitions.

Furthermore, the Holy Spirit makes intercession for us before the Father to have our needs met. The Holy Spirit knows what we need, and He stands as our prayer partner to remind the Father of anything we forget to mention. Suppose, for example, I pray to the Father for a needed suit jacket and pants, but I forget to mention the shoes. The Holy Spirit will say, "Father God, Hakeem, Your son, needs new shoes, too!" Do you see that the Holy Spirit is interceding "for" me just has He has previously interceded "with" me?

Partnering with the Holy Spirit will help you receive things from the Father that you desperately need. The Holy Spirit gives us words to say in prayer because He speaks God's language! John 15:7 (KJV) declares: "If ye abide in me, and my words abide in you, ye shall ask what ye will, and it shall be done unto you."

God is in search of prayer warriors who will stand in the gap for each other. Partnering with others and the Holy Spirit will cause you to reap divine blessings and protection from unseen dangers. It will create a prayer network that reinforces the will of God coming to pass in your life.

In summary, I want to remind you that prayer changes everything! Yet so many things fight for our attention and get in the way of communicating and connecting with God. Prayer is not something to do when life happens and you have exhausted all your options. Seek the Lord in prayer daily, use these ten prayer secrets and look for divine breakthrough.

If you want to continue with the daily prayer activations for chapter 10 at this time, please turn to Days 28 through 30, found in part 2 of this book.

If you are entering the thirty-day devotional study, please continue with part 2, "30 Days of Prayer for Breakthrough." Each devotional contains reflection questions, declarations, Scriptures for study and activations.

PART 2

30 DAYS *of* PRAYER *for* BREAKTHROUGH

PROTECT YOUR PASSION

Never lagging behind in diligence; aglow in the Spirit, enthusiastically serving the Lord.

ROMANS 12:11 AMP

At the very moment we decide to lose our passion, zeal or even enthusiasm for the things we love, our perspective or vision loses its divine focus. The devil knows this, and he loves nothing better than an apathetic Christian. Protect the flames within! This zeal of the Lord is a consuming fire within you; guard it ferociously at all costs, realizing that it is the enemy's target. Take time to protect your passion.

—— REFLECTION ——

▶ On a scale of 1–10, with 1 being "cold" and 10 "hot," where do you place your sense of passion in prayer right now? Is it growing, diminishing or about the same as it has been for a while?

▶ Think of a time when your passion in prayer was high. What circumstances caused this, and what was the result?

▶ Think of a time when your passion in prayer seemed diminished or low. What circumstances caused this, and what was the result?

1. God is lighting my heart with His fire to pursue my purpose passionately.

2. God is directing my steps so that I am accurately in His will for my life.

3. I will fulfill my divine calling with the right heart and motives.

4. I declare that I will use everything the Father has placed in my hands to honor Jesus.

5. I will purposely accomplish all that God has called me to accomplish in my generation.

Father God, give me clarity about my purpose so that I can possess a renewed sense of love for what You have called me to do. Show me areas of improvement for spiritual enrichment and empowerment. Ignite me with fresh passion to fulfill my destiny and Your purpose. In Jesus' name, Amen!

SCRIPTURE STUDY: Matthew 6:21; 1 Corinthians 9:24–27; 10:31

ACTIVATION

▶ What is one primary "passion killer" you have experienced? Determine to stand against it now in Jesus' name. Write down any ways you can be on guard against this obstacle to godly passion.

▶ Ask God to show you one specific, practical thing you can do to ignite or increase your passion. Write it down and put it into practice in some way today.

PURPOSE-DRIVEN PASSION

Many are the plans in a person's heart, but it is the LORD's purpose that prevails.

PROVERBS 19:21

God will fuel your dreams with the breakthrough power necessary for you to excel in life. At the same time, it is the plan of the enemy for you to run on empty hopes, dreams and aspirations. Every decision you make points you either in the right direction or in the wrong direction. God wants you to make destiny decisions that are Holy Spirit driven. You can have confidence knowing that God will empower you with a sense of purpose, direction, meaning and security.

—— REFLECTION ——

▸ On a scale of 1–10, with 1 being "not satisfied," 5 "satisfied" and 10 "extremely satisfied," what is your level of satisfaction with your life?

▸ What drives you or moves your heart? Think about the things you are most passionate about. This can help you see the passions God has put into your heart.

▸ What are some things that fill your heart with holy discontentment or frustration? This can also help you see the passions God has put into your heart.

1. I am more than a conqueror in Christ Jesus (see Romans 8:37).

2. I will not embrace or settle for anything that is not part of God's plan for my life.

3. I will keep a positive outlook on life and pursue my purpose relentlessly regardless of the odds (see Job 42:2).

4. I decree and declare that my purpose in Christ Jesus will not be altered, forfeited or confused by the enemy, in Jesus' name.

5. I will arise and shine in God's glory (see Isaiah 60).

Father, show me Your purpose for my life and what steps I need to take to walk out that calling. I ask for the drive, wisdom and inspiration to finish what I have started. Break the cycle of stagnation and fuel me with a purpose-driven plan of action, grace and power from the Holy Spirit. In Jesus' name, Amen!

Scripture Study: Proverbs 20:5; Romans 8:28; Philippians 2:12–13; 2 Timothy 1:9

── Activation ──

▸ Observe what you are most passionate about (the passion God has given to you) and write down what you feel is God's primary purpose for your life.

▸ Write down a few short-term and long-term goals that will help you obey God's calling. Pray for wisdom, and write down one simple way to move toward accomplishing those goals today.

Passion on Purpose

The purposes of a person's heart are deep waters, but one who has insight draws them out.

Proverbs 20:5

God desires for your passion to become your purpose so that over time it will ultimately become your occupation. What you are most passionate about will turn out to be part of your purpose and destiny. Never allow your discontentment or frustration to get the best of you. Employ and ignite your passion while working your purpose in God to the fullest. Work hard, sacrifice, dream big and love what you do, and in return there will be a great reward.

---- Reflection ----

▸ What unique gifts and abilities has God given you? This will help you identify your passion and purpose.

▸ What experiences in your life are really fulfilling to you? What are your deepest desires? This can help you see the passions God has put into your heart.

▸ What legacy do you want to leave? What would you do with your life if you had all the money you needed? This can assist you in passionately pursuing your purpose.

1. God will help me fulfill my purpose (see Philippians 2:13).

2. God works through my difficulties to fulfill His purpose in my life (see Romans 8:28).

3. I will not miss what God has purposed me to do.

4. I will serve the purposes of God passionately in my generation (see Acts 13:36).

5. I will live life on purpose and purposely leave a legacy for those I love.

> *Father,* give me the wisdom and knowledge needed to execute *Your plan and purpose in my life daily. Show me how to connect with and relate to others who can help me maximize my full potential and purpose in You. Burn in my heart a desire never to give up and always to finish what You started. In Jesus' name, Amen!*

SCRIPTURE STUDY: Job 42:2; Ecclesiastes 3:1; Isaiah 46:10–11; Jeremiah 29:11; 32:19

— ACTIVATION —

▸ What are some challenges, hardships and difficulties you have overcome or are in the process of overcoming? Write down how you overcame or how you will overcome them.

▸ Ask God to help you identify areas that distract, hinder and block you from pursuing your passion and purpose. Pray for wisdom, and do one thing today to move toward accomplishing those goals.

Expect the Unexpected

You know that the testing of your faith produces perseverance.

JAMES 1:3

God does not want us to be surprised by the unusual events that occur in our lives. He desires that we walk by faith and not by what we know or what we can visibly see before us. Live life anticipating the impossible becoming possible by the power of believing! Anticipating the unexpected by faith is key to your breakthrough. The possibilities of God become the normalcy of the believer. Your faith brings pleasure to God, and your obedience brings treasures from God.

Reflection

▸ Do you feel that your faith is growing or diminishing or has it leveled off in your life?

▸ Are you someone who believes that God has an ultimate plan and purpose for you? Do you have faith in yourself? Why or why not?

▸ Think about those times when your faith was strong and times when it was weak. What were the challenges you faced that caused this, and what was the outcome?

1. I will walk by faith and not by sight (see 2 Corinthians 5:7).

2. By faith I will receive what I ask God for in prayer (see Matthew 21:22).

3. I will live by faith because I am the righteousness of Christ (Romans 1:16–17).

4. I will anticipate my breakthrough by faith in God's power (see James 1:3).

5. I will activate mountain-moving faith to receive my breakthrough (see 1 Corinthians 13:2).

Father, give me the faith required to envision what You desire for me to obtain. Show me how to reach out by faith to visualize the breakthroughs You have already planned for my life. Break the fear of the unknown and instill in me a heart to live by faith to expect the things You can accomplish only through me. In Jesus' name, Amen!

Scripture Study: Mark 9:23; Romans 10:10; Ephesians 3:16–17; Hebrews 11:6

— Activation —

▸ What areas in your life cause your faith to be shaken? Today, ask God to give you Holy Spirit power to overcome fear, doubt and unbelief.

▸ Highlight areas of your faith that you presume to be weak. Ask the Father in prayer to reveal specific, practical things you can accomplish today to increase your faith to receive breakthrough.

FAITHING IT

So then faith comes by hearing, and hearing by the word of God.

ROMANS 10:17 NKJV

God is pleased by our faith, and without faith our works are lifeless. The enemy desires for us to live by fear and not by faith. Faith is like the air we breathe: Just because we cannot see it does not mean it does not exist. It is like not seeing the wind even though we can feel it, or not seeing electricity but seeing the light. Living by faith will house the breakthrough power of God—and its effects will be seen visibly in your life!

— REFLECTION —

▶ What people, places or things have become faith blockers keeping you from hearing God's voice daily?

▶ How has your faith been tested? What does the Bible say about faith in these areas of testing?

▶ What areas of your faith do you want to grow? How can you draw near to God in those areas?

1. I will stand firm in the faith, and be on guard, courageous and strong (see 1 Corinthians 16:13).

2. I will walk in faith, hope and love, focusing especially on the greatest of them all: love (see 1 Corinthians 13:13).

3. I will fight the good fight of faith (see 1 Timothy 6:12).

4. I will overcome and replace fear with faith that has been tested and tried (see 1 Peter 1:7).

5. I will listen with ears of faith to the message of God's Word for my life (see Romans 10:17).

Father, I pray for the power of the Holy Spirit to equip me to endure seasons of testing of my faith. Reveal to me specific areas of distraction to overcome so that I can live victoriously. Teach me how to please You by faith and how to draw closer to You. In Jesus' name, Amen!

SCRIPTURE STUDY: John 1:12; Romans 5:1; Peter 1:8–9; 1 John 5:41

ACTIVATION

▸ Write down one primary fear in your life. Today in prayer ask God for the grace and boldness to step out in faith to conquer that fear.

▸ What are some practical faith goals you want to see happen in the coming weeks, months or years? Today, write down a simple action plan of faith to fulfill these goals God has given to you.

ADVANCE BREAKTHROUGH

Now faith is confidence in what we hope for and assurance about what we do not see.

HEBREW 11:1

In life you will experience new opportunities. Along the way the enemy will set up a sudden detour to reroute you onto a path of confusion or bewilderment. He wants to break you down in your pursuit. God, however, uses this as a "defining moment" in your life and makes a way of escape for you. Your breakthrough is just ahead. It is soon within your reach. See it and seize it!

―――――――― REFLECTION ――――――――

▶ What promises from God are you waiting to receive? This will help you identify what to pray for specifically.

▶ In what areas of your life, including new opportunities, do you feel the most resistance from the enemy? Knowing this will give you clarity about what to fight for relentlessly in prayer.

▶ Identify areas of need for yourself or others that can come to fruition only with God's supernatural assistance and provision. This will help you pray bold, faith-filled prayers to break invisible blockages.

1. God is the Lord of the breakthrough in every area of my life (see 2 Samuel 5:20).

2. God gives me supernatural faith to receive my inheritance in Christ (see Ephesians 1:11–17).

3. I will stay alert, knowing that God will provide a way of escape from the snares of the enemy (see 1 Corinthians 10:13).

4. I decree and declare that I will receive a double portion of everlasting joy (see Isaiah 61:7).

5. Because I rely on God, I expect perpetual breakthroughs in my life—in Jesus' name!

Father, grant me divine strategies and insight to receive turnaround breakthroughs in my life and in the lives of those I am praying for. Show me in Your Word how to war against invisible enemies effectively. Empower me by the Holy Spirit to pray fear-shattering prayers that get instantaneous results. In Jesus' name, Amen!

SCRIPTURE STUDY: Isaiah 43:19; 54:17; Ephesians 3:20; James 1:3

— ACTIVATION —

▸ Today in prayer ask God to show you what steps to take to position yourself for breakthrough. Write down those steps, along with the results you anticipate, and put a check mark beside each one as it occurs.

▸ Recall any times when you took a detour set up by the enemy. Write down the thoughts you had at the time that caused you to take your eyes off your promise. Use this to stay alert as you pursue your advance breakthrough.

PRAY BY EXAMPLE

May your Kingdom come soon. May your will be done on earth, as it is in heaven.

MATTHEW 6:10 NLT

The greatest test of life that the enemy will challenge is your obedience to God. Take care not to cheat yourself out of passing the exam that comes to test your faith. Arise in prayer and set the bar high for others to follow. Jesus became the ultimate prayer example and model for you to conquer life's fears, oppositions and obstacles. Obedience to God is proof of your commitment, faithfulness and love for Him. Your obedience will open unexpected doors of blessing, favor and opportunity.

REFLECTION

▸ What does the word *prayer* mean to you? A set time and place to meet God? Speaking throughout the day to your heavenly Father and listening for His voice? Do you feel that you live a life of prayer?

▸ Think about things that keep you from praying effectively and consistently. What do you experience when you do or do not pray consistently?

▸ What do you say when you pray? Are your words generic or specific? Knowing this will help you think more precisely and listen more intently when speaking with the Lord.

PRAYER DECLARATION

1. With Jesus as my example, I will express complete, personal and heartfelt prayers.
2. As I pray, I draw close to God and He draws close to me.
3. I will remain faithful, loyal and committed to staying in God's presence in prayer.
4. I will walk in obedience to God's call on my life.
5. I will love the Lord with all of my heart and mind, and with all of my strength.

Father God, teach me how to pray in accordance with Your will. Show me clear steps to take today to fulfill Your purpose for my life. It is my desire to walk in obedience to Your Word. Reveal specific areas in my prayer life that need an upgrade. In Jesus' name, Amen!

SCRIPTURE STUDY: Deuteronomy 28:1; 1 Kings 2:3; Luke 9:23; John 14:23

ACTIVATION

▸ Today find a Scripture that speaks to you personally. Meditate on it, and then express the Scripture in prayer to God. After a few minutes, write down what you believe God is saying to you from that Scripture.
▸ Ask God to show you specific areas of focus to enhance and revitalize your prayer life. Write them down and practice them.

DISCIPLED BY PRAYER

The secret things belong to the LORD our God, but the things that are revealed belong to us.

DEUTERONOMY 29:29 ESV

Jesus' model of prayer set the precedent regarding how to communicate with God. Living in God's presence brings refreshment and breakthrough! You are called to practice His presence. God has secrets that He discloses only to His children. Do you know your true identity in Christ? God's Word declares: "You are a chosen people, a royal priesthood, a holy nation, God's special possession, that you may declare the praises of him who called you out of darkness into his wonderful light" (1 Peter 2:9).

--------- REFLECTION ---------

▸ On a scale of 1–10, 1 being "not satisfied," 5 "satisfied" and 10 "extremely satisfied," how satisfied are you in your relationship with God?

▸ Are you excited when you pray? Why or why not? This will help you remove anything that makes prayer boring.

▸ Do you feel that for the most part you pray according to God's will? Why or why not?

1. God is my Father, and I treat His name with respect.

2. God will ignite the passion within me to communicate with Him consistently in prayer.

3. God will give me insight about removing anything that blocks His will from being perfected in my life.

4. I choose to walk in total obedience to God's will for me.

5. I will practice what I pray.

Father, I repent of anything that has become a substitute for You in my life. Thank You for the outline in prayer that Jesus gave His disciples. Help me to fulfill Your will and Word. Keep me from walking in ignorance. Impart to me the divine wisdom necessary to accomplish Your purpose today. In Jesus' name, Amen!

SCRIPTURE STUDY: Matthew 6:13; Luke 11:1–4; 22:42; John 4:34; 5:19–20

ACTIVATION

▸ Observe what you most want to change about your prayer life. Write down what you believe it is, and pray about it today with all your heart until you feel a desire to take a different approach concerning it.

▸ Ask God in prayer today for ways to make your relationship with Him exciting, satisfying and more creative.

BLUEPRINT OF PRAYER

"For I have come down from heaven, not to do My own will, but the will of Him who sent Me."

JOHN 6:38 NASB

Prayer is not for the faint of heart but for those who have chosen to be lovers of God's presence and have laid down their lives as living sacrifices. With prayer, sweat and tears, Jesus gave us a heavenly template for communicating and executing God's will here and now. The enemy knows that if your prayers ascend to heaven, his every unseen plot, plan and strategy will be exposed. God's blueprint for prayer is classified intelligence to those who are called coheirs with Christ.

—— REFLECTION ——

▸ How do you posture yourself when you pray (sit, kneel, etc.)? Do you pray silently in your head or out loud with your voice? Do you prefer short or long prayers?

▸ Do you use a prayer list, ask the Holy Spirit to lead you or both? What are the differences in these two experiences? Do you get the same results?

▸ Have you ever used the Lord's Prayer as an outline for your prayers? What does it mean to you to seek His Kingdom?

1. I will adopt, customize and implement the prayer model and protocol that Jesus set for me.
2. I will pray for myself, and pray for others more than myself.
3. I will take the limits off prayer in order to experience God's power.
4. I will spend more time in God's presence to receive my breakthrough.
5. I will overcome spiritual opposition in prayer.

Father, I want to pray effective prayers. Reveal to me the people You want me to pray for so they will receive their blessings and breakthroughs. Give me a list of things You desire for me to overcome. I thank You that the Holy Spirit leads me in prayer. Grant me wisdom and insight to pray with power and authority. In Jesus' name, Amen!

SCRIPTURE STUDY: Matthew 6:9–13; Mark 1:35; Luke 5:16; John 11:41–42; Hebrews 5:7

— Activation —

▶ Write down a few things you could do differently before, during and after you pray that will excite your prayer life. Step out in faith to pray whatever God places in your heart to pray (friend, family, coworker, business, etc.)

▶ The next time you pray, do something different or unpredictable that you have not done before in prayer.

Spiritual Renewal

When I wept, and chastened my soul with fasting, that was to my reproach.

PSALM 69:10 ASV

One effective weapon against the forces of evil is to join fasting with prayer. The enemy entices us with worldly pleasures, desires and temporal things that act as forbidden fruit. You do not have to succumb to lust of the eyes, lust of the flesh and the toxic offers of the devil. The power of fasting will help you break old habits, overcome irresistible appetites and draw you closer to God. This is your time of spiritual awakening and renewal. *Note: Always check with your health-care provider before undertaking any rigorous change in diet.*

—— REFLECTION ——

▸ What freedom have you encountered through the breakthrough power of God? What impact did that have on you afterward?

▸ How do you measure your holiness and closeness with God? By comparison with those around you, or by what is written in the Word of God?

▸ How do you currently handle unwanted temptations, lusts, thoughts, appetites or cravings?

1. I will not give in to ungodly lust, appetite or craving.
2. As I fast, I will draw closer to God's presence.
3. I will grow daily in my hunger for the power and presence of God.
4. My fasting will cause me to experience supernatural breakthrough and freedom.
5. I will conquer and overcome every stronghold of the enemy that has kept me bound.

Father, give me divine strength to fight the war over my flesh. Show me the type of fast You require of me. Impart to me the endurance to finish that fast as I pray. Revive and equip me with Holy Spirit power. In Jesus' name, Amen!

Scripture Study: Ezra 8:21–23; Psalm 35:13–14; Matthew 6:16–18

— Activation —

▸ Is there an ungodly lust, appetite or craving that you struggle with? Write it down and ask God to help you break through and sever its hold on you.

▸ Think about specific areas that hinder your relationship with God and your breakthrough. Ask God what type of fast to do to impart strength, wisdom, insight and endurance to help you overcome.

BREAKTHROUGH FAST

So we fasted and earnestly prayed that our God would take care of us, and he heard our prayer.

EZRA 8:23 NLT

God responds to those who abstain from unhealthy desires. Fasting brings empowerment to our prayer lives. Humility, clarity, insight, revelation, direction and wisdom come through fasting and prayer. The enemy wants to highlight your weaknesses, ungodly proclivities, struggles, pain, past failures and difficult circumstances. God desires for you to depend solely on Him for your spiritual freedom. Fasting is not about emptying our stomachs but rather about refilling our spirits with God's desires.

— REFLECTION —

▸ Is there an area in which you are currently experiencing physical fatigue, weakness, struggle or indecisiveness? God could be highlighting an area to target with fasting and consistent praying until breakthrough occurs.

▸ Are you facing spiritual blockage, hindrance, setback or unexplainable resistance? Consider how joining a fast with your prayers might help release the supernatural assistance from the Lord that you need.

► If you are fasting and praying and are still experiencing a delay in answered prayer, think about Daniel, whose prayers went unanswered for 21 days while a spiritual battle ensued.

Prayer Declaration

1. I will hunger and thirst after righteousness and will be satisfied (see Matthew 5:6).
2. I will not live by bread alone but by every word that comes from God's mouth (see Matthew 4:4).
3. I will humble myself before the Lord with fasting, and He will answer my prayers.
4. I will detox with a fast to rid myself of spiritual and physical toxicity.
5. I will overcome the plots and hidden plans of the enemy set against me.

Father, grant me endurance while I fast and pray. Break me free from every unhealthy, toxic, unproductive pattern, habit or cycle. Renew and restore all that is my portion in You. Give me a blueprint to follow to maintain my healing, deliverance and breakthrough. By Your power I am free and liberated today. In Jesus' name, Amen!

SCRIPTURE STUDY: Isaiah 58:5–12; Joel 1:14; 2:12

Activation

► Today choose one unhealthy habit, pattern or hindrance that you will address with prayer and fasting. Ask God to break its power and influence over your life.
► Monitor your progress by writing down how you feel after you have fasted and prayed.

CLOSENESS WITH GOD

"But even now," declares the LORD, "return to me with all
your heart—with fasting, crying, and mourning."

JOEL 2:12 GW

The Father longs to have oneness with those who are His. We
live in a world of indulgence, greed, pride, fame and self-
gratification—not self-denial. Fasting will turn your attention away
from self and toward a victorious lifestyle in God's presence. Fasting and prayer heighten your spiritual sensitivity—awareness that
compels you to draw closer to the Father's heart. You are not just
giving up your will regarding your actions but also surrendering
your life, sacrificing to the One who gave His life for you.

—— REFLECTION ——

▸ What gray areas of self-discipline do you want to tackle in
  your life? Fasting will help you focus on those areas and bring
  resolution to them.

▸ How well are you hearing God's voice and direction? Fasting
  and prayer will unclog your spiritual hearing to give you wisdom, clarity and direction.

▸ In what way do you want to deepen your spiritual walk and
  relationship with God?

1. I want my life to be a living sacrifice, holy and acceptable unto God (see Romans 12:1).
2. I will draw near to God, and He will draw closer to me (see James 4:8).
3. When I succumb to wrongful or sinful behavior, I will confess this before God, for He is just to forgive me of all unrighteousness (see 1 John 1:9).
4. I will not be sidetracked by anything that is pulling my attention away from the Lord.
5. I want to hear the voice of God daily in my life.

Father, open my heart to hear Your voice. Give me confirmation when I have obeyed Your direction. I want a deeper walk with You daily. Assist me as I fast to draw deeper and closer to Your presence. I want to stay in right standing and fellowship with You. Father, fill me with more of Your love. In Jesus' name, Amen!

SCRIPTURE STUDY: Mark 9:29; 2 Peter 3:14; 1 John 1:8–10

── ACTIVATION ──

▸ Ask the Father to show you how you can walk closer with Him.
▸ While you are fasting, write down what God is impressing upon your heart to stop, change or start.

TIME TESTED

Until the time came to fulfill his dreams, the LORD tested Joseph's character.

PSALM 105:19 NLT

Waiting on the Lord to fulfill His dream, word and will over your life can feel like an eternity. Have faith in God's timing. He is making you ready for what is yet ahead. Time may feel as though it is not on your side. Never grow tired of doing what is good. At just the right time you will reap a harvest of blessing if you do not give up (see Galatians 6:9). You are being processed by time. Your readiness for breakthrough will depend on how you persevere in the midst of adversity, opposition and setbacks. Pass the test of time!

REFLECTION

► What prayers are you waiting for God to fulfill? How long have you been waiting? Have you grown weary, impatient or frustrated? Have you stopped praying about something you have been waiting for? If so, why? God may be testing your endurance, patience, character and level of faith.

► How ready do you feel to receive what you are waiting for from God?

1. God gives me words of wisdom while awakening me morning by morning to open my understanding to His will (see Isaiah 50:4).

2. I will wait for the God of my salvation, and He will hear me (see Micah 7:7).

3. God is good to me as I seek Him patiently with my heart (see Lamentations 3:25).

4. I will be still and know that He is the God of my life (see Psalm 46:10).

5. I will rejoice in hope and be patient in tribulation but continue to pray (see Romans 12:12).

Father, teach me how to wait on Your promises. Help me with a plan of action while I wait on Your word to be fulfilled. I do not want to waste time praying for something that is not Your will. Confirm what is not and what is. Strengthen and equip me to fulfill only Your will. In Jesus' name, Amen!

SCRIPTURE STUDY: Colossians 1:11; James 1:12; 2 Peter 3:9

ACTIVATION

► Ask God to show you specifically what is His will and write it down.

► While you wait on God to answer your prayers, reflect on the prayers He has already answered and give Him praise.

THE APPOINTED TIME

> "The vision is yet for the appointed time; it hastens toward the goal and it will not fail. Though it tarries, wait for it; for it will certainly come, it will not delay."
>
> HABAKKUK 2:3 NASB

God's dream for your life has a due date to be birthed. In the fullness of time it will happen. It is the strategy of the enemy to cause you to abort God's promise, purpose and destiny. Resist him and he will retreat. Your dream will come forth full term! Sarah and Abraham at an old age had a word that they would conceive a son. At the appointed time they birthed God's promise—Isaac.

REFLECTION

▸ What is your vision or mission? What is the time frame for its fulfillment?

▸ Have you given up on what God has promised you? If so, why? Do you believe God will fulfill His word in your lifetime?

▸ Think again of the specific things you are expecting from God. Are they things that will serve God's purpose in your life? Knowing this will help you examine what is required for the moment while waiting on other things.

PRAYER DECLARATION

1. I will not grow weary in well-doing and will not faint waiting on God's promises (see Isaiah 40:31).
2. I will wait patiently and serve the vision of God over my life until He fulfills it.
3. I will not allow my faith to be shaken or broken while waiting on God's timing.
4. I will not get out of God's will and lose faith regarding what God has promised me.
5. I will live to see and enjoy God's promises in my life.

Father, give me strength and endurance to wait on Your promises. Help me formulate and execute short- and long-term goals to work on while I wait for You to answer my prayers. Impart the gifts of the Holy Spirit. Activate faith in me to wait on the vision and mission to come to pass in Your timing. In Jesus' name, Amen!

SCRIPTURE STUDY: Psalm 37:7; Acts 1:4; James 5:11

ACTIVATION

▸ Pick one aspect of your vision that you can work on and make progress on today.
▸ Pray for the ability and power of the Holy Spirit to overcome setbacks, hindrances, distractions and delays in your life.

REDEEMER OF TIME

Make good use of every opportunity you have, because these are evil days.

EPHESIANS 5:16 GNT

Opposition comes to test your patience. Use every opposition as a moment of opportunity given to help you overcome anything that is keeping you from fulfilling your God-given destiny. Breakthrough comes when you have relentless faith to penetrate every barrier, resistance and blockage. When you lose track of time, God will redeem, restore, reset and restart your time again! He controls the clock of life. God will accelerate time for you because of your faith to wait on His promises. The enemy wants you to waste time and live life unfulfilled. God, however, will recycle time for you to fulfill the dreams of heaven.

REFLECTION

▸ Have you ever missed a great opportunity? How did you feel? This can assist you in prayer to ask God for help with good time management and preparation.

▸ Think of an occasion when you missed something important because you were late or forgot what time it was. Did you see God redeem the time on your behalf?

▶ How much do you value being on time? What are the benefits?

1. God will redeem the time I have lost and will restore the years I have lost (see Joel 2:25).
2. My times and future are in the hands of the Lord (see Psalm 31:15).
3. I will love and be patient while waiting on God's timing (see Psalm 130:5–6).
4. I will be steadfast, immovable, always abounding in God's work (see 1 Corinthians 15:58).
5. I declare that I am blessed because of my steadfastness, love and patience in God (see James 5:11).

Father, allow me not to miss any of Your opportunities. Help me to strategize a plan and a schedule to implement in order to follow them through. Redeem the time that I have lost. Forgive me if I have failed to move by faith in what You have called me to do. Ignite in me a passion for everything You love. Give me supernatural grace and ability to seize every "God moment." In Jesus' name, Amen!

SCRIPTURE STUDY: Proverbs 14:29; 16:32; Romans 8:25

ACTIVATION

▶ Write down one specific thing you want God to help you with concerning time and seeing His opportunities for you.
▶ Pray and ask God for discernment and wisdom to know what doors of opportunity to accept or reject.

FRIENDSHIP OF GOD

"You are My friends if you do what I command you."
JOHN 15:14 NASB

God desires a one-of-a-kind friendship with you. He is very picky when it comes to those He considers His friends. Faith and obedience are the "God criteria" for a healthy, loving, admirable and faithful partnership. The enemy is an antagonist against those who are lovers of Christ. God is a jealous God and is a protagonist of those He calls His trusted admirers. You do not have to fight for God's attention! Your faith, trust and obedience in God have already sealed your mutual friendship.

—— REFLECTION ——

▸ How often do you talk with your close friends? What do you have in common with them? How can you communicate with God on a similar personal, intimate and relatable level?

▸ How transparent, open and responsive are you as a friend? How do your close friends make you feel when they speak? How do they feel when you speak?

▸ Do you believe you are God's friend? Explain your answer.

1. I will not fear but will walk in faith in Him because He is with me (see Isaiah 41:10).

2. God is gracious and slow to anger. He shows compassion and love toward me (see Psalm 86:15).

3. God is for me; who can be against me? I am a protected friend (see Roman 8:31–32).

4. Nothing can separate me from the love of God (see Romans 8:38–39).

5. I will be strong and courageous because God will not leave me or abandon me (see Deuteronomy 31:6).

Father, I desire to open my heart to You to fill it with Your love. Cover and protect me when I am vulnerable and weak. Give me a heart like King David, who was a man after Yours. Reveal to me what it takes to walk by faith and obedience to become the trusted and loyal friend You desire today. In Jesus' name, Amen!

SCRIPTURE STUDY: Psalm 27:4; John 15:14–15; Romans 5:8

ACTIVATION

► What is one area in your life that you want to be more open and honest about with God and others?

► Ask God what act of faith He wants you to do today to bless someone in need.

HOLY COMPANIONSHIP

But now you must be holy in everything you do, just as God who chose you is holy.

1 PETER 1:15 NLT

Prayer and faith keep your friendship with God in good standing. A holy companionship with the Lord is not changing what you do per se, but ultimately, over time, changing your perspective and attitude toward what you do. God has chosen you not because you are holier than others, but because your faith in Him to become an obedient and faithful servant in His sight qualifies you as His friend. True worship in spirit and truth is what the Father searches the earth for. Be like David, a man after God's heartstrings!

REFLECTION

▸ What does it look like to have an actual friendship with God? Does that excite, challenge, stretch your faith—or all of the above?

▸ What is your next step to start a new journey in faith with God?

▸ Do you love worshiping God? If so, what do you feel or sense in His presence?

1. I believe God and will walk righteously as a friend of God (see James 2:23).

2. I want to be justified by my good works and not just faith alone (see James 2:24).

3. I will not break my covenant relationship with God.

4. I will keep an open line of communication with God in prayer daily.

5. I will worship God in spirit and truth, as this is what He longs for from me.

Father, I want a one-on-one close friendship with You. Share with me what is on Your heart so that I can obey You by faith. If I fall short of Your glory, Father, please restore me once again. Lead me, Holy Spirit, to walk in obedience and live a holy life pleasing to God. In Jesus' name, Amen!

SCRIPTURE STUDY: Psalm 23:1–6; 91:1, 4; Hebrews 10:22; James 2:23

ACTIVATION

▸ Write down what you feel friendship with God requires.

▸ Talk to the Holy Spirit about your present spiritual condition or your desire to be His friend.

FAITHFUL CONFIDANTS

A faithful man will abound with blessings.
PROVERBS 28:20 ESV

Love is what exemplifies a true, intimate relationship between two friends. God is a faithful confidant to those who love Him and are faithful in obedience no matter what. His steadfast love toward you extends beyond the heavens, and His faithfulness endures to all generations (see Psalm 36:5; 119:90). The Lord knows how to handpick His faithful comrades and acquaintances. The enemy knows how to sow seeds of fear, doubt, unbelief and distrust in God's ability to answer your prayers. True admirers of God will not take the bait. Love conquers fear! "There is no greater love than to lay down one's life for one's friends" (John 15:13 NLT).

—— REFLECTION ——

▶ How can you draw closer to your all-powerful Friend?

▶ Abraham's faith and obedience pleased God. What does being faithful and obedient mean to you? Do you have any expectations from God? If so, what are they?

▶ How do you want to live your life if you and God are friends?

1. I will be faithful with what belongs to another person so God can give me my own (see Luke 16:12).

2. I will be faithful unto death so that God will give me a crown of life (see Revelation 2:10).

3. God is my protective shield and buckler (see Psalm 91:4).

4. God will not allow me to be tempted beyond my ability (see 1 Corinthians 10:13).

5. God chose me first before I chose Him (see John 15:16).

Father, help me walk in the fear of the Lord daily, which is the beginning of wisdom. Help me, Father, to take my place in a consistent, faithful and viable love relationship that is acceptable and pleasing in Your sight. Break me free today from every unfaithful, unproductive and distracting thought or action. Thank You for Your patience with me, and help me to do things right. In Jesus' name, Amen!

Scripture Study: 1 Samuel 26:23; 2 Chronicles 16:8–9; Matthew 25:21; Luke 16:10

—————— Activation ——————

► Identify unchecked areas in your relationship with God that need attention and make proper alignments in your obedience.

► Consider how God has been faithful to you. Thank God in prayer for His faithful friendship and favor in your life.

INVISIBLE FRIENDS

For he will command his angels concerning you to guard
you in all your ways.

PSALM 91:11 ESV

Angels are inseparable friends that God sends to impart
strength, protection and a message of hope to anyone who
will involve them in their daily activities. Angels are our invisible
best friends. God allows companionship with angels because He
sends them to take personal care of each of us. When the enemy
sends an uncalculated attack to stop our prayers from coming to
pass, warring angels of God show up disguised and unannounced
to defeat our invisible enemies. Activate your angelic friends!

— REFLECTION —

▸ What experience do you have with angels?

▸ What is the purpose of angels in your life?

▸ How can you partner with angels to experience sudden spiritual and financial breakthroughs and victories?

1. Angels will help me break through in times of hardship, struggle and financial lack.

2. Angels will assist me in fulfilling the purposes of God for my life (see Daniel 10:14).

3. Angels are personal administrators and dispensers sent by God to bless me.

4. Angels listen to the voice of the Lord and execute His will in my life.

5. Angels take interest in my daily affairs and help me to overcome life problems.

Father, show me how to partner with angels in fulfilling Your purpose daily in my life. Send Your ministering angels to reveal Your divine message and blueprint for me to implement and obey. I know that we are not to worship angels, but give me language in prayer to ask You how to send them in times of need. Deploy Your angels to cover me today to live victoriously. In Jesus' name, Amen!

Scripture Study: Psalm 103:20; Daniel 3:28

——— Activation ———

▶ In what areas do you currently experience resistance or drought? Pray that God will send His angels to bring you provision, increase and supernatural favor.

▶ Spend some time worshiping Jesus, which attracts angelic activity in your life.

ANGELIC GUARDIANSHIP

> "Behold, I send an angel before you to guard you on the way
> and to bring you to the place that I have prepared."
>
> EXODUS 23:20 ESV

Jesus understood the power of angelic guardianship and protection. At His word He could summon an innumerable number of them. God has sent angelic watchers for surveillance, protection and guidance for your footsteps along the journey He has predestined for you. You will not lose sight of what your destiny entails. Angels are equipped to win the spiritual battle of evil coming against you. There is a restraining order filed against the enemy over your life. If he trespasses or violates it—angels will come to the rescue!

REFLECTION

▸ Was there a time when you found yourself in a life-threatening situation or needed emergency help? How did you feel afterward? Could it be that God sent angelic help to save, protect and bless you?

▸ Have you received unexpected blessings, favor and opportunities? Could it be that God sent angels to assist you?

▸ How can you cooperate with God's ministering angels to advance the Kingdom of God?

1. God has sent angelic reinforcement to make the crooked places straight.

2. God has unleashed angels to protect my assets, property, family, business, ministry and life.

3. God has sent invisible warriors to bring divine blessings, favor and opportunities.

4. God has sent angels to strengthen, warn, guide, guard and share prophetic messages.

5. God has sent angels of financial blessings and daily provision into my life.

Father, guide me in all Your ways. Send angels to watch over me and those I love. Teach me how to partner with angels so I will not miss what You have ordained for me. I want to learn more about these ministering spirits. Share insight with me today concerning them so that I will not be ignorant of their assignments in my life. In Jesus' name, Amen!

SCRIPTURE STUDY: Exodus 23:20–23; Daniel 6:22; Hebrews 1:7

— ACTIVATION —

▶ Ask God in prayer to send angelic protection over everything you own or value and everyone you love.

▶ Write down all your financial needs and ask God for supernatural provision today.

Angels on Assignment

Who maketh his angels spirits; his ministers a flaming fire.

PSALM 104:4 KJV

A ngels are assigned to you and will come to your rescue when you are in distress. There is an invisible force working for you behind the scenes. God knows when you are in need of His help. You do not have to fight spiritual battles alone. Arise and know that there are more with you than against you! Activate your faith today to call on God's ministering spirits—angels!

REFLECTION

▸ What stories have you heard about angels on assignment?

▸ What was the effect when angels showed up?

▸ Ponder the people, places and things in your life that need God's protection.

PRAYER DECLARATION

1. Angels are assigned to my prayers today.

2. Angels are executing the purposes of God for my life.

3. Angels are ministering supernatural strength to me when I am weak.

4. Ministering angels are protecting, encouraging, guiding and bringing answers of purpose and hope (see Exodus 23:20).

5. Ministering angels of God are watching over and surrounding me today (see Psalm 91:11–12).

Father, I ask You to send Your angels before me to make the crooked places straight. I know Your angels respond only to Your voice and Your words. Teach me how to partner with Your word and will for my life and send angels to assist me in fulfilling them. When I am weak, confused, lost and afraid, Father, dispatch Your angels to guide, strengthen and protect me in all my ways. In Jesus' name, Amen!

SCRIPTURE STUDY: Psalm 34:7; Luke 4:10; Hebrews 1:14

──────── ACTIVATION ────────

▸ Ask God in prayer to send angelic assistance to areas of need in your life.

▸ Think about areas in which you notice spiritual and personal conflict, hardship, opposition and stagnation. Today, pray for God to impart wisdom, clarity and insight into those areas and to send angels of breakthrough with divine answers.

FORGIVE TO BE FORGIVEN

> Bear with each other and forgive one another if any of you has a grievance against someone. Forgive as the Lord forgave you.
>
> COLOSSIANS 3:13

God's love is like spiritual *kryptonite* against the force of unforgiveness. It takes a strong individual to apologize and even a stronger individual to forgive. God wants us better, not bitter. One of the greatest gifts you can give is to forgive yourself and to forgive everyone else. Never allow bitterness, resentment, unforgiveness, past offenses and unresolved issues to imprison your potential in God. Forgiving others ensures God's forgiveness. Forgiveness is the key to a life of freedom, healing, happiness, joy and peace in the Holy Spirit!

--- REFLECTION ---

▸ What is your definition of *forgiveness*? Is there any current unresolved offense, hurt, resentment, bitterness or unforgiveness in your life? If so, why have you not let go?

▸ Jesus died and forgave us for our sins on the cross. What does His act of forgiveness mean to you? Are you open to forgiving and loving others after being hurt?

▸ Think about a time you asked for forgiveness from someone or needed to forgive. How did you feel before, during and after? Reflect on both ends of forgiveness.

1. I will not hold on to grudges and past offenses or harbor unforgiveness in my heart.
2. I will not allow bitterness, resentment and unresolved issues to hold me hostage.
3. I will make the decision today to display God's love and forgive others.
4. I will forgive others so that God can forgive me of my offenses or trespasses.
5. I will continue to practice forgiveness until I am totally free.

Father, reveal to me those I need to forgive so that I can experience freedom and breakthrough. Give me a heart to love others, and give me a step-by-step plan today to learn how to love and forgive. Heal me from any unresolved hurt of the past. Impart Your love supernaturally that I might forgive. In Jesus' name, Amen!

SCRIPTURE STUDY: Matthew 18:21–22; Ephesians 4:32; Colossians 3:13

── ACTIVATION ──

▸ Ask God to identify every individual you have not forgiven.
▸ Write down their names and identify what is keeping you from forgiving them.

POWER TO PARDON

Be angry and do not sin; do not let the sun go down on your anger, and give no opportunity to the devil.

EPHESIANS 4:26–27 ESV

Jesus is the greatest example of what forgiveness looks like: He died for the sins of humanity on the cross. Jesus' blood of atonement is the legal reparation for God to forgive us. Because it effected forgiveness for the sins of the world, it allows everyone who asks to receive the Father's free offer of salvation. Further, it marks the standard for walking in forgiveness toward ourselves and others every day. The enemy wants to indict you on all charges of past and present offenses on the premise of unforgiveness. Activate the power to silence the accuser of the brethren and choose to forgive yourself and others. To forgive someone will ultimately bring reconciliation and restoration, not retribution and retaliation.

— REFLECTION —

- ► Who has betrayed, hurt or offended you—either someone you love or someone you do not know?
- ► How often should you forgive someone? Is there a limit or time frame for you to ask for forgiveness or accept someone's forgiveness? Why?

- What have you learned about forgiveness through past experiences that can help resolve issues more quickly in the future?

— PRAYER DECLARATION —

1. I will quickly resolve any past issues or offenses regardless of who is at fault.
2. I will release myself from any harbored resentment, which is unhealthy and toxic.
3. I will continue to love those who hate me and pray for those who use me.
4. I will walk in God's love and forgiveness so that I am blessed and free.
5. I will always forgive those who offend me, even if they are not sorry.

Father, I want to be an example of Your love. Teach me more about Your grace so I may learn the importance of forgiveness. Put people on my heart to love, pray and forgive. I want to experience the power of reconciliation, restoration and personal revival. Sever me from recurring offenses in my life and heal me. In Jesus' name, Amen!

SCRIPTURE STUDY: Isaiah 43:25; Matthew 18:21–22; Luke 17:3–4; Ephesians 4:26–27

— ACTIVATION —

- Observe areas in your life that have little-to-no breakthrough.
- Write down those areas and ask God to show you if unforgiveness is blocking your answer.

FORGIVE TO FORGET

"I will be merciful toward their iniquities, and I will remember their sins no more."

HEBREWS 8:12 ESV

Love and forgiveness are the prerequisites for true repentance. God's love will shatter the strongholds of fear, doubt, hatred, dissension, division and unforgiveness. The wise know how to forgive; the ignorant forget to forgive; and the immature refuse to forgive. But the one who has God's love can forgive and forget! Forgiving someone does not leave you powerless but powerful in making the decision to free yourself and others from the hurt, the pain and the memory. Forgiveness does not erase the past but has the potential to change the present and create the future you have always wanted.

— REFLECTION —

▸ If you still experience pain when you remember offenses against you, either you have not genuinely forgiven or you need personal healing. Where are you still experiencing pain?

▸ Job forgave his friends and God restored him. What kind of restoration do you need?

► Forgiveness is not a feeling but a decision. What is keeping you from forgiving enemies or friends who have wronged you?

1. God will heal my heart from past hurts when I forgive.
2. God is teaching me how to extend mercy and maintain my personal healing as I forgive.
3. I will not allow the past to dictate my future by holding on to past or present grudges.
4. I will daily experience total healing, restoration and financial breakthrough.
5. I will no longer hold people or myself responsible for past hurts done to me.

Father, empower me to exonerate and forgive those who have offended or hurt me. Give me a step-by-step resolution plan of action in Your Word to forgive and heal. Help, equip and educate me, Holy Spirit, to love, pray and forgive others as Christ forgave and loved me. In Jesus' name, Amen!

SCRIPTURE STUDY: Romans 12:19; Philippians 3:13; 1 Peter 4:8

— ACTIVATION —

► Ask God to finish the process of healing to get past the past and embrace the future as you forgive.
► One by one and out loud, completely forgive yourself and others who have hurt you.

Praise Power

Be exalted, O Lord, in your strength! We will sing and praise your power.

Psalm 21:13 esv

Praise is a "God shield" of protection and a weapon against the enemy who comes to silence your voice and bring disharmony. Allow your song to become a love melody and symphony before the Lord. He desires to hear a new song of praise sung with breakthrough power. Defeat worry, anxiety, oppression, stress and setbacks with thanksgiving; it is the enemy of discontentment, discouragement and dissatisfaction. Praise power breaks ungodly cycles, resistance and strongholds of the enemy. Get ready to lift your voice like a trumpet! A sound of freedom and victory is in your mouth. The power of your breakthrough is in the strength of your praise.

Reflection

▸ What is your typical remedy when you feel restricted, bound, overwhelmed, depressed, stressed or oppressed?

▸ Paul and Barnabas were imprisoned unjustly, and they prayed and sang praises to God at midnight. What does the spiritual weapon of praise look like in your situation right now?

► What are some favorite worship or praise songs that change your atmosphere when you play them?

──────── PRAYER DECLARATION ────────

1. God will inhabit, live in and reside in my praise, which will bring breakthrough.
2. God will break open opportunities on my behalf as I praise Him with my mouth.
3. God will use my praise to lift Him up, and He will scatter my enemies.
4. When I praise Him, God will deliver my soul when I am in need (see Jeremiah 20:13).
5. God will use my praise as a sound of liberty and victory.

Father, ignite my passion to praise You in the midst of warfare. Revive me when I am low, broken, perplexed and oppressed. Today give me the zeal of the Lord to praise You unashamedly that I may be set free. Anoint and activate my praise to break the power of fear, and arm me with the power of praise to become victorious. In Jesus' name, Amen!

SCRIPTURE STUDY: Psalm 34:1–4; 101:1; Daniel 2:23; James 5:13

──────── ACTIVATION ────────

► Ask God to give you a new song to sing praises to Him to bring healing and deliverance.
► Find your favorite Scripture and sing it (add a spontaneous melody) as a song of victory.

PRAISE BREAK

> O sing to the LORD a new song, for He has done wonderful things, His right hand and His holy arm have gained the victory for Him.
>
> PSALM 98:1 NASB

When you are at a breaking point, break out with breakthrough praise. Do not permit the devil to win on the battlefield of your mind. Pierce through the darkness with a break-of-day song of praise! Let God hear the lamb (the sacrifice) in your worship and the lion (the power) in your praise. "For the LORD your God is living among you. He is a mighty savior. He will take delight in you with gladness. With his love, he will calm all your fears. He will rejoice over you with joyful songs" (Zephaniah 3:17 NLT).

—— REFLECTION ——

► How might you express your praise to God in a way that is out of your comfort zone? Singing, laughing, dancing, bowing, spinning, shouting, clapping and rejoicing are biblical ways to praise. Do not limit yourself.

► When is the last time you broke out of a place of comfort or stagnation? Identify limitations so you can praise your way out.

► What results do you see when you choose to focus on the opposite of how you are feeling?

1. I will praise God continually, and He will help me win spiritual battles daily.

2. I will exalt God in my praise, and He will work wonders and miracles in my life.

3. God created me to praise and worship Him, and He will break open unmovable strongholds and barriers.

4. I will dance, sing, shout, praise and play songs of freedom and breakthrough.

5. I will use my praise as a two-edged sword that will help me break past resistance.

Father, allow my praise to You to be an atmosphere changer. Give me new songs to sing when I am depressed, lonely, stressed, confused and overwhelmed. Help me to pray and praise like Paul and Barnabas in order to encounter total freedom and breakthrough. Empower, equip and anoint me with Holy Spirit boldness and courage to praise You any time. Holy Spirit, shatter spiritual chains in my life today. In Jesus' name, Amen!

Scripture Study: 2 Chronicles 20:22; Psalm 149:6; Acts 16:25–26

— Activation —

▸ Write down in prayer what you desire to encounter when you break out in praise.

▸ Think about where you want to see breakthrough, and then take a break and activate your praise to God. You might, for example, replace sadness with gladness in your praise.

Praise Anthem

> "He is your praise and He is your God, who has done these great and awesome things for you which your eyes have seen."
>
> DEUTERONOMY 10:21 NASB

Fill your lips daily with continuous praise for God that will push back the barrage of persecution, opposition and attacks from the enemy. Your praise anthem will become the song of healing, deliverance, victory, blessings, restoration and supernatural breakthrough. Whenever unknown, unseen and unpredictable forces of evil surround you, and you do not know what to do, shout with a voice of triumph of praise! God promises to undertake a sneak attack against your enemies, and they will turn in confusion and defeat themselves because of your praise weapon.

—— REFLECTION ——

- ▸ Are you introverted or extroverted? Do you prefer to praise God in private or publicly or both. Why?

- ▸ When you do praise God, how do you feel? How excited are you to experience a new level of praise in God's presence?

- ▸ Consider that the enemy is defeated when God arises in your praise (see 2 Chronicles 20:22). When all the forces of evil, confusion, doubt and unbelief come against you, and the pressures of life happen, praise is the answer to breaking through the darkness.

Prayer Declaration

1. My praise will silence the enemy when he comes to block my blessings from God.
2. My praise and worship in prayer will create an atmosphere for miracles to happen.
3. My praise and thanksgiving unto God will not be muzzled, silenced or restricted.
4. My praise will declare God's righteousness daily, and freedom will be released.
5. My praise and thanksgiving will be radical for the glory of God.

Father, help me to teach others about Your glory as I praise You daily. Give me boldness to step out of my comfort zone and to bless You with the fruit of my lips and the expression of my body. Impart to me wisdom and understanding to discern when to praise You in my darkest moments. Accept my daily praise anthem. In Jesus' name, Amen!

Scripture Study: Psalm 40:3; 42:5; Isaiah 12:5; Jeremiah 20:13

Activation

▸ Write down every good thing you want to say to God and activate your praise.

▸ Ask God in prayer how He wants you to praise Him and by faith do it!

Holy Spirit Synergy

"I also tell you this: If two of you agree here on earth concerning anything you ask, my Father in heaven will do it for you."

MATTHEW 18:19 NLT

Holy Spirit synergetic praying creates a powerful vitality of God's presence in your life. The power of agreement will create a force shield that is impenetrable for the enemy. You do not have to fight alone! The Holy Spirit has been sent to become your prayer partner. He is your advocate, champion, consultant and advisor. Your faith is voice-activated when you pray with others and in the power of the Holy Spirit. Heaven will invade your life through this prayer partnership.

—— REFLECTION ——

▸ Jesus was the earthly model of one who has a lifestyle of prayer and partnership with the Holy Spirit. How do you want to partner with the Holy Spirit?

▸ What does connecting with the Holy Spirit feel like to you? What have you discovered that breaks your connection?

▸ Why is it easy to neglect the Holy Spirit? What happens when we pay attention to Him?

1. The Holy Spirit will give me daily access to the Father to hear His voice.

2. The Holy Spirit will help me know the mind, will and purpose of God.

3. The Holy Spirit will make intercession for me and help me break through.

4. The Holy Spirit will lead, guide, direct, correct, equip, educate and empower me.

5. The Holy Spirit will help me know how to pray when I do not know how.

Father, I want a deeper walk and relationship with the Holy Spirit. Show me how to partner with Him. Holy Spirit, anoint me with fresh oil to be equipped with Your glory. Activate supernatural power to help me break through every day in prayer. In Jesus' name, Amen!

SCRIPTURE STUDY: John 5:14–15; Romans 8:23–30; Jude 20

— ACTIVATION —

▸ Ask God in prayer to help you connect more deeply with the Holy Spirit.

▸ Write down specific things you need the Holy Spirit to assist you with, and then tell Him.

POWER OF UNITY

> With all prayer and petition pray at all times in the Spirit, and with this in view, be on the alert with all perseverance and petition for all the saints.
>
> EPHESIANS 6:18 NASB

When we pray together, we stay together. God knows that at times you may not know what to pray for. This is when the Holy Spirit takes full advantage of the opportunity to communicate your heart to God's ears. The deliberate plan of the enemy is to bring discord, disharmony and dissention. Counteract his plan by unifying yourself with the Holy Spirit and other believers so God can command blessings to be supernaturally released into your life. God answers prayers of agreement.

REFLECTION

▸ What does *unity* mean to you?

▸ How do you demonstrate to the Lord and in your relationships that you are a team player?

▸ What has been your experience with a prayer partner or someone you know who was interceding and fighting for you? Do you have a prayer partner now? What has been the benefit?

1. By the Holy Spirit I will continue to know and pray for God's will for my life (see Romans 8:27).
2. I will continue to partner with others in prayer to experience breakthrough.
3. The Holy Spirit will give me a new prayer language to communicate with God.
4. The Holy Spirit will lead me into all truth and the wisdom of God (see John 16:13).
5. The Holy Spirit will give me words to say in difficult and trying times (see Luke 12:12).

Father, send me prayer partners to pray for and with me. Identify areas in my life that need prayer support so that I can overcome obstacles and break through. Enhance my life with the right people who can pray, fight and touch Your will for my life daily. Bless me to win. In Jesus' name, Amen!

SCRIPTURE STUDY: 2 Chronicles 7:14; Acts 12:5–18; Galatians 6:2; James 5:16

— ACTIVATION —

▸ Consider how any disunity you experience is the enemy's attempt to disrupt a relationship that could create breakthrough if you prayed together.
▸ Consider with whom you feel most united. Call that person today and agree with him or her in prayer for breakthrough.

CORPORATE PRAYING POWER

You also [join] in helping us through your prayers, so that thanks may be given by many persons on our behalf for the favor bestowed on us through the prayers of many.

2 CORINTHIANS 1:11 NASB

There is nothing more powerful, effective and remarkable than when believers come together to pray in one accord and unleash the agenda of heaven on earth. Corporate prayer and intercession have the ability to shake the foundations of hell and open the heavens over your life for perpetual breakthrough, healing, deliverance and miracles. The enemy wants you to become the weakest link. Never break rank! Join forces with the Holy Spirit and others to encamp around the enemy of your destiny, and he will wave the white flag of surrender.

—— REFLECTION ——

▸ The leadership team of the New Testament Church called an emergency prayer meeting to intercede for Peter, and he was later released supernaturally from jail. Have you been part of a group standing in the gap to pray for someone? What was the result?

- ▸ Where are the weak links in your relationships with others that you have seen the enemy try to exploit?
- ▸ Are you connected to a church, prayer community or ministry that believes in corporate prayer and intercession?

PRAYER DECLARATION

1. God will send me faithful prayer partners to help me resist the enemy.
2. God will empower me with a church, ministry and friends who will intercede for me.
3. God will continue to give me prayer support through other believers and leaders.
4. God is sending me other Christians who will fight for me in prayer when I cannot.
5. God will use the power of agreement in prayer to release divine blessings.

Father, connect me with a group that prays effectively, by the Holy Spirit. Outline for me a daily plan to pray for other people's needs. Empower me today to pray strategic prayer that changes things for me and for others. In Jesus' name, Amen!

SCRIPTURE STUDY: Joel 1:14; Philippians 1:19; 1 Timothy 2:1

ACTIVATION

- ▸ Ask God whom you can trust for prayer about personal areas of your life. Reach out to that person, ask for prayer and believe together for breakthrough.
- ▸ Pray for any weak relationships you have that hinder the power of corporate prayer.

My Notes

MY NOTES

MY NOTES

My Notes

DR. HAKEEM COLLINS is an empowerment specialist, respected prophetic voice, life coach and sought-after transformational leader. He is known for his keen accurate prophetic gifting, breakthrough prayers and supernatural ministry. He is the author of several books, including the bestselling *Heaven Declares*. He has been featured on many television and radio programs and networks including Sid Roth's *It's Supernatural*, the Word Network, GOD TV, Elijah Streams, TBN, *Atlanta Live* and Cornerstone TV. He is a regular contributor to *Charisma* magazine and the Elijah List. Dr. Collins holds a master's degree in Christian leadership and honorary doctorates in both philosophy and divinity. He is the founder of Champions International, the Prophetic Academy and Revolution Network based in Wilmington, Delaware, where he resides.